REVIEWS FOR
Mr. President, The Class Is Yours:
Jimmy Carter's Sunday School Lessons in Washington D.C.

"When I was pastor of First Baptist D.C., I heard story after story about Jimmy Carter teaching Sunday School in the balcony, but this book helps me get close not only to the history, but to the experience of being in President Carter's Sunday School class. It's a good place to be."

THE REVEREND JIM SOMERVILLE
PASTOR, FIRST BAPTIST CHURCH
RICHMOND, VIRGINIA

"Reading *Mr. President* is the next best thing to being in Jimmy Carter's class. These lessons happened in a specific time and place but will always be relevant to any reader's life."

THE REVEREND DEBORAH COCHRAN
ROCKVILLE, MARYLAND

"In *Mr. President, The Class Is Yours*, the intense and oft-over-looked personal nature of Jimmy Carter's faith is revealed as leaven for his public role forging the common good."

THE REVEREND CHUCK BOOKER
PASTOR, BETHESDA PRESBYTERIAN CHURCH
BETHESDA, MARYLAND

"The book is full of instances ... where Carter would give an understated nod to the weight of his day job before pivoting, with reverence, to the biblical text of the week."

CRAIG NASH
SENIOR EDITOR, GOOD FAITH MEDIA
WACO, TEXAS

ALSO BY CHRISTI HARLAN

Mr. President, The Class Is Yours:
Jimmy Carter's Sunday School Lessons in Washington, D.C.

NORMAL LIVES

*President Jimmy Carter
and His Church*

CHRISTI HARLAN

Christi Harlan Media LLC
Washington, D.C.

Published by Christi Harlan Media LLC

www.christiharlanwriter.com

christi@christiharlanwriter.com

FIRST EDITION

Paperback ISBN: 979-8-9902263-2-6

E-book ISBN: 979-8-9902263-3-3

Library of Congress Control Number: 2024920457

Printed in the United States of America

Cover Photo courtesy of the Jimmy Carter Presidential Library

Photo of Christi Harlan by Jay Brousseau

Cover Design by MiblArt / www.miblart.com

Book Editing and Design by Booktique Consulting / www.booktiqueconsulting.com

Copyediting by Diane Porter

Proofreading by Deb Collins

❧ Created with Vellum

To Joe Murray, my editor, publisher and friend.
In appreciation for his faith in me and in the man upstairs.

CONTENTS

THE TEACHERS

THE LESSONS IN THE BALCONY

INTRODUCTION

I was barely a year out of college when my mom helped me move from a small city in East Texas to Dallas.

"I'm never doing this again!" she exclaimed after the last box hit the floor of my new apartment. "You newspaper reporters—all you have is paper!"

Guilty. I love my notebooks, I love editing drafts on paper, and I really love seeing my words typeset and printed. Put me in a room with boxes and drawers of documents and newspaper clippings, and I'm happier than a pig in, well, *Charlotte's Web*.

I was one happy pig in February 2023 when a friend unlocked the inner door to the most valuable archives of our church, the First Baptist Church of the City of Washington, D.C.—Jimmy Carter's church for the four years he was in the White House.

I knew the church had some recordings of Carter teaching Sunday School while president, and I knew we had a fair amount of newspaper clippings from the time. I was surprised by the number of recordings—14, including the original reel-to-reel tapes—and the quantity of material that had been saved by the church and its members, from church newsletters and Sunday bulletins to clippings of newspaper and magazine articles about the Carters.

Other artifacts from Carter's time at First Baptist D.C. actually fell out of file folders, including the small blue cards the Carters filled out when they presented themselves for membership. A sheaf of handwritten pages turned out to be the recreation of an usher's diary, in which he collected all of his entries about interacting with the Carters—assembled as Parkinson's disease began to cripple his hands.

What follows isn't a narrative. It's largely an anthology of my reporting on the church and the people who passed through or near it between 1977 and 1981—members, visitors, reporters, protesters and, of course, the President of the United States.

This is also a scrapbook. The reporters before me who covered Jimmy Carter's time at First Baptist had a perspective I cannot replicate. Many of those accounts—particularly in the defunct *Washington Star* and the newsletters of First Baptist and the DC Baptist Convention—aren't digitized and risk being lost.

In the course of my own reporting, I found some gems, including an oral history interview containing Carter's thoughts on Harry S. Truman, another president who worshipped at First Baptist D.C. Other pieces of the story came inexplicably from nowhere, such as the night I met Jim LeBrecht on a street in Washington, D.C., and learned that First Baptist was in the documentary he co-directed, *Crip Camp*. The film tells the story of the disability rights advocates who occupied a federal building in San Francisco in April 1977 and sent a contingent to President Carter's church to get his attention. Spoiler: They didn't get in the door.

Four years aren't many out of Jimmy Carter's 100 or First Baptist's 222. But between January 1977 and January 1981, thousands of people found their way to First Baptist D.C. I went into journalism to avoid math, so I won't try to solve that equation.

For me, it adds up to a volume of stories about people who came to my church. For some, church wasn't part of their normal lives; they were there out of curiosity or to make a statement. For many others, church was part of their normal lives. President Jimmy Carter was one of those.

Christi Harlan
Washington, D.C.
November 2024

ABOUT THIS BOOK

The title, *Normal Lives*, comes from the remarks President Jimmy Carter made at the annual banquet of his Sunday School class at the First Baptist Church of the City of Washington, D.C.:

"You have made our lives normal lives. You have given us stability in a position that is inherently sometimes unstable. A president of our country can be an isolated person. You have taken us in, and we are indebted to you."

The book is a collection of short pieces intended to shed light on the church that embraced Carter as a person, not a president, and Carter's reciprocal affection for a church that was a haven from his cares of office. The first section, "The Introit"—named for the short choral piece sung to open a worship service—gets the President and his family inside First Baptist, an effort that started with competition among churches months before he was elected.

The next three sections are named for the old children's game where you lace together the fingers of both hands and recite: "Here is the church; here is the steeple. Open the door and see all the people."

The chapters in "The Church" describe the history and structure of the sanctuary where President Carter worshipped at least 75 times during his 48 months in office. "The Steeple" is a surprise. The chapters in "The People" tell the stories of some of the groups and individuals who encountered or attempted to encounter President Carter at church.

The companion volume to this book, *Mr. President, The Class Is Yours*, contains transcripts of 14 Sunday School lessons that President Carter taught to the Couples Class at First Baptist D.C. The section titled "The Sunday School Class" tells the story of the group of working professionals—women and men—who gathered for Bible study every Sunday and welcomed a new two-career couple in January 1977.

"The Teachers" describes Carter's remarkable rapport with lead teacher Fred Gregg. The two Southerners were gifted at both Bible study and insult comedy. Only a few of the funny bits appeared in *Mr. President, The Class Is Yours* because I needed room to explain that Fred Gregg was comfortable enough to needle the President of the United States, and POTUS gave as good as he got. Their exchange about the last book of the New Testament could easily be titled "Abbott and Costello Do Revelation." Do not be drinking a carbonated beverage when you read it.

The final section of this book, "The Lessons in the Balcony," contains the backstories of some of those lessons, including the Sunday that President Carter brought a Ukrainian Baptist pastor to class after negotiating his release from Soviet custody.

A couple of style notes: This book quotes heavily from news coverage, speeches and other material from the late 1970s. Some words and phrases accepted then are not acceptable today. I use the original language because I'm a reporter. For excerpts from the usher's diary and other sources, I generally use the original capitalization and punctuation.

With few exceptions, I use First Baptist D.C. to refer to my church —President Carter's church. The official name is The First Baptist Church of the City of Washington, D.C. It's a mouthful to say and expensive to print over and over. You'll know who we are, and you're welcome anytime.

In this book, I commit three sins of deliberate omission. First, I say little about Amy Carter, who was nine years old when she was baptized at First Baptist D.C. She was an active participant in her Sunday School class and good friends with church members of her age. But she was a child, and I am following an old journalism rule to take great care when reporting about a child. That said, her baptism was widely covered in the press, and the story of her dealing with a loose tooth in the middle of worship was too good to pass up.

The second omission concerns names. Correspondence and other church records contain the names of some church visitors and members. I made every effort to locate those people to ask permission to quote from their writings and use their names. People I couldn't find aren't named. I also omit the names of protesters arrested for disrupting worship at First Baptist D.C. I couldn't find any news reports of how the charges were adjudicated. A clerk for the D.C. Superior Court told me the court records for the 1970s had been destroyed in 2012. Consider the omission of the protesters' names an act of forgiveness from this church member.

Late in the writing of this book, I learned that reports of President Carter's characterizations of certain Gospel passages during two of his Sunday School lessons caused pain among Jews and Christians in Israel and the United States. I am neither a historian nor a theologian, and I did not feel confident in my ability to tell that story without the depth of reporting I devoted to the rest of the book. No audio recordings of the lessons exist in the church archives, nor are they part of *Mr. President, The Class Is Yours.*

I am grateful beyond words for the opportunity to share these stories. I hope you enjoy reading them as much as I enjoyed writing them.

THE INTROIT

THE CAMPAIGN

Two Washington churches have taken keener than usual interest in presidential politics this year.

First Baptist Church and Calvary Baptist Church are about equal distance from the White House, where each hopes to recruit a new parish family come next January.

MARJORIE HYER

WASHINGTON POST, AUGUST 1, 1976

For Protestant churches in Washington, D.C., few things inspire as much missionary zeal as the election of a new president who is a known churchgoer. The hand of Christian fellowship was vigorously extended to Barack Obama, Bill Clinton and, unsurprisingly, Jimmy Carter.

Carter's Christian faith was an integral part of his campaign for the presidency in 1976. It got a lot of longtime political reporters into the candidate's home church, Plains Baptist Church, in Georgia, including Carl P. Leubsdorf, whose coverage of the 1972 presidential campaign for the Associated Press got him into the classic account of political press, *The Boys on the Bus* by Timothy Crouse.

In an email exchange, Leubsdorf was asked: Was it possible to cover Jimmy Carter as a politician without covering his religiosity?

"Good question," he replied. "I don't think so. It both affected how he lived his life and his political appeal. It was part of his appeal in some places and a disadvantage elsewhere. ...

"And I really think it was part of what motivated him. Unlike some other presidents, his regular Sunday church attendance was real, not political. But he also believed in the separation of church and state, which is why he went to a church off campus instead of having services, like Nixon, in the White House."

Those off-campus churches in Washington swung into missionary mode early in 1976 in an effort to put a pew under a president. Less than three weeks after Carter secured the nomination at the Democratic convention in New York City, the religion editor for the *Washington Post*, Marjorie Hyer, was handicapping the race for Carter's membership at two D.C. churches.

"Jimmy Carter has promised that if he is elected, he will worship regularly in a Baptist church near the White House," Hyer wrote. "To the Rev. Dr. Charles A. Trentham, that can only mean First Baptist six blocks up 16th Street from the North Portico of the executive mansion.

"To the Rev. Dr. [George W.] Hill, the nearest Baptist church is clearly Calvary, six blocks out G Street from the White House East Gate."

In interviews with Hyer, Trentham was clearly eager to welcome Carter as a member. Hill was more laid-back:

"[Carter] was quoted to me as saying he would attend the Baptist church closest to the White House. If you look at a map," [Dr. Hill] said with a laugh, "you'll find we're a couple of hundred yards closer [than First Baptist]."

Hyer noted that First Baptist had an ace up its sleeve when it came to snagging Carter's membership:

"First Baptist began sweet-talking Carter way back in the primaries, when the church's pastor emeritus, the Rev. Dr. Edward Hughes Pruden, met the candidate at a Kiwanis luncheon in Raleigh, N.C."

Pruden's son, Edward H. Pruden Jr., filled out the story:

In the summer of 1976 when former Governor Jimmy Carter of Georgia was running for president, he spoke at the Kiwanis Club in Raleigh, North Carolina. My parents had retired to Raleigh in 1969 after 33 years in Washington. Dad had a very active retirement during their decade in Raleigh. ...

He was a member of the Kiwanis Club and it was well known that he had been President Truman's pastor in Washington. When the club leaders learned that Jimmy Carter was coming to speak, they asked Dad to provide the invocation.

When Dad got up to give the invocation, he began by saying, "Before offering our invocation, I would like to give Governor Carter a picture postcard of the First Baptist Church in Washington. It is located just six blocks from the White House and is the church where President Truman and his family attended. If he [Carter] is elected president, we hope he will consider attending as well." Then my dad offered the invocation.

Carter thanked Dr. Pruden for the postcard and said, "When I was elected governor, I visited an older lady in our home church in Plains. I mentioned to her that we would attend a church in Atlanta but would keep our letter at our home church in Plains. The lady said to me, 'No Jimmy, that's not right. When you move your cook-stove, you move your letter!' "

———

The *Washington Post*'s coverage of the campaign for Carter's church membership—a full three months before the presidential campaign would end—inspired a member of another D.C. church to write to the newspaper's editor:

"I read with amusement Marjorie Hyer's article August 1 on the rival claims of First Baptist and Calvary Baptist to Jimmy Carter's possible attendance, because I had already sinned in my heart by coveting him as a member of National Baptist at 16th and Columbia NW. ...

"The congregation is a yeasty mix of suburban whites, downtown blacks and Spanish-speaking (for whom there is a Spanish-language service). There is a warm feeling of community. In spite of its neighborhood-oriented character, however, it remains the National Baptist Church of the entire nation. If Jimmy Carter doesn't give us a drop-by, I am going to brood."

THE PRAYERS

*Save him from his friends, who in misdirected devotion, would make his
way easy but compromising. Deliver him from the colleagues who, in the
name of the party or even the nation, would persuade him from the holy
path of righteous leadership for all people.*

ROBERT CAMPBELL

GENERAL SECRETARY OF THE AMERICAN BAPTIST CHURCHES

PRE-INAUGURAL PRAYER

When First Baptist D.C. held pre-inaugural prayer services for
Jimmy Carter in January 1977, the president-elect still hadn't
announced which church he would join.

Pre-inaugural services are no guarantee that the host church will
become the president's home church. Bill Clinton, for instance,
attended a single prayer service at First Baptist before his inauguration in 1993 but never returned, choosing to regularly attend
Foundry Methodist Church, a block north on 16th Street.

President-elect Carter attended two services at First Baptist: one
the evening before the inauguration and a more private service at 9
a.m. the day of. At both services, the opening hymn was "O God,
Our Help in Ages Past."

The program for the service on Wednesday, January 19, 1977, listed Scripture readings identified as "The Bible Speaks" on four civic topics: government leaders, people in authority, government and citizenship. Four prayers were spoken between Scripture readings: for the new President, for the cabinet, for the nation and for Christian citizens. (That last prayer was inexcusably exclusionary, even for 1977.)

The call to worship came from Psalms 33:12-22:

12 Blessed is the nation whose God is the Lord; and the people whom he hath chosen for his own inheritance.

13 The Lord looketh from heaven; he beholdeth all the sons of men.

14 From the place of his habitation he looketh upon all the inhabitants of the earth.

15 He fashioneth their hearts alike; he considereth all their works.

16 There is no king saved by the multitude of an host: a mighty man is not delivered by much strength.

17 An horse is a vain thing for safety: neither shall he deliver any by his great strength.

18 Behold, the eye of the Lord is upon them that fear him, upon them that hope in his mercy;

19 To deliver their soul from death, and to keep them alive in famine.

20 Our soul waiteth for the Lord: he is our help and our shield.

21 For our heart shall rejoice in him, because we have trusted in his holy name.

22 Let thy mercy, O Lord, be upon us, according as we hope in thee.

The Reverend Bruce Edwards, then pastor of Carter's longtime church home, Plains Baptist Church, offered the first Scripture readings entitled "The Bible Speaks on Government Leaders" with verses from Psalms, Romans and 1 Timothy. (Less than a month later, Edwards would resign the pulpit in Plains, Georgia, over resistance to welcoming Black people to the church.) The reading started with Psalms 72:1-2, 12-14:

1 Give the king thy judgments, O God, and thy righteousness unto the king's son.

2 He shall judge thy people with righteousness, and thy poor with judgment. ...

12 For he shall deliver the needy when he crieth; the poor also, and him that hath no helper.

13 He shall spare the poor and needy, and shall save the souls of the needy.

14 He shall redeem their soul from deceit and violence: and precious shall their blood be in his sight.

It continued with Romans 13:3-5:

3 For rulers are not a terror to good works, but to the evil. Wilt thou then not be afraid of
the power? do that which is good, and thou shalt have praise of the same:
4 For he is the minister of God to thee for good. But if thou do that which is evil, be afraid;
for he beareth not the sword in vain: for he is the minister of God, a revenger to execute
wrath upon him that doeth evil.
5 Wherefore ye must needs be subject, not only for wrath, but also for conscience sake.

And ended with 1 Timothy 2:1-2:

1 I exhort therefore, that, first of all, supplications, prayers, intercessions, and giving of
thanks, be made for all men;
2 For kings, and for all that are in authority; that we may lead a quiet and peaceable life in
all godliness and honesty.

First Baptist's pastor emeritus, Edward Hughes Pruden, offered
the closing prayer that day: "Go with us, Lord, that we may be
committed to the kind of righteousness which exalts a nation; that
we may be involved in the quality of citizenship that is worthy of the
Gospel of Christ; that we may be faithful in witness and ministry,
hallowing your name."

The Carters, vice president-elect Walter Mondale and Mondale's
wife and family were back at First Baptist at 9 a.m. Thursday,
January 20, 1977. Mondale's father-in-law, the Reverend Dr. John
Maxwell Adams, a Presbyterian minister, conducted the service.

"President Carter requested of our church a private service, that
he and our new Administration's leaders might offer sincere and
personal worship to Almighty God just prior to Inauguration," the
First Baptist Church News reported January 26, 1977. "Our congregation, thereby, has given to our new President a gift for which we may
rightly feel joy."

Despite the hospitality extended by First Baptist, the Carters were
noncommittal about their choice of churches. After the Inauguration
Day service, spokespeople for the Carter family insisted to the *Washington Post* that no decision on the president's membership had been
made among the Baptist churches that had extended invitations to
the president-elect, including First Baptist and Calvary Baptist, as

well as National Baptist Memorial Church and Riverside Baptist Church in southwest Washington.

The headline on the *Post* story the next day was straight out of a campaign: "1st Baptist Leads Race For Carter."

THE INVITATION

[A]t the close of the 11 a.m. worship service Dr. Charles A. Trentham, pastor of the church, gave the traditional Southern Baptist invitation for visitors to bring their letters of transfer if they cared to join the church.

WILLIAM F. WILLOUGHBY

WASHINGTON STAR, JANUARY 24, 1977

Baptists, like all Christians, base their religion on concepts that are sometimes recited as the "mystery of our faith": Christ has died, Christ has risen, Christ will come again. For other matters, like eligibility for church membership, Baptists rely less on faith and more on documentation.

So it was for a family attending worship at the First Baptist Church of the City of Washington, D.C., on January 23, 1977. At the end of the service, the pastor issued the "invitation," or altar call, encouraging anyone who wanted to join the church to walk to the front of the sanctuary.

The family stood and walked forward, where ushers gave them little blue cards to write their names and check the means by which they sought membership. The young girl indicated she was seeking baptism; the adults checked the line for "transfer of letter" from a prior church.

The pastor introduced the family to the congregation, asking, "All you who join the pastor in recommending them to the membership committee raise your hand," reported William F. Willoughby in the now-defunct *Washington Star* newspaper.

It was up to the membership committee of First Baptist D.C. to affirm the bona fides of the new members, which included obtaining a letter of recommendation from their prior church.

A small white card arrived at First Baptist D.C. in May 1977. In handwriting and typewriting, the church clerk of Plains Baptist Church in Plains, Georgia, attested that "Pres. and Mrs. Carter, Chip (James Earl III) and Caron Carter" were members in "regular standing ... and, in compliance with your request, are given this letter cordially recommending them to your fellowship."

With those formalities—a public expression of intent, a background check and a letter of recommendation—Jimmy Carter, the 39th President of the United States, officially became a member of the First Baptist Church of the City of Washington, D.C.

———

In the end, it wasn't proximity to the White House or the entreaties of the pastors that swayed Carter's choice of a church. The president-elect had launched his own intelligence-gathering operation that turned out, unintentionally, to be undercover:

"We decided to join the First Baptist Church, primarily because [my son] Chip and [his then-wife] Caron, during the pre-inauguration days, had attended several of the churches and found this one to be both warm and friendly, even when the people there didn't know who our children were. Also, Amy decided to become a member of the church and to be baptized there."

FROM THE ARCHIVES

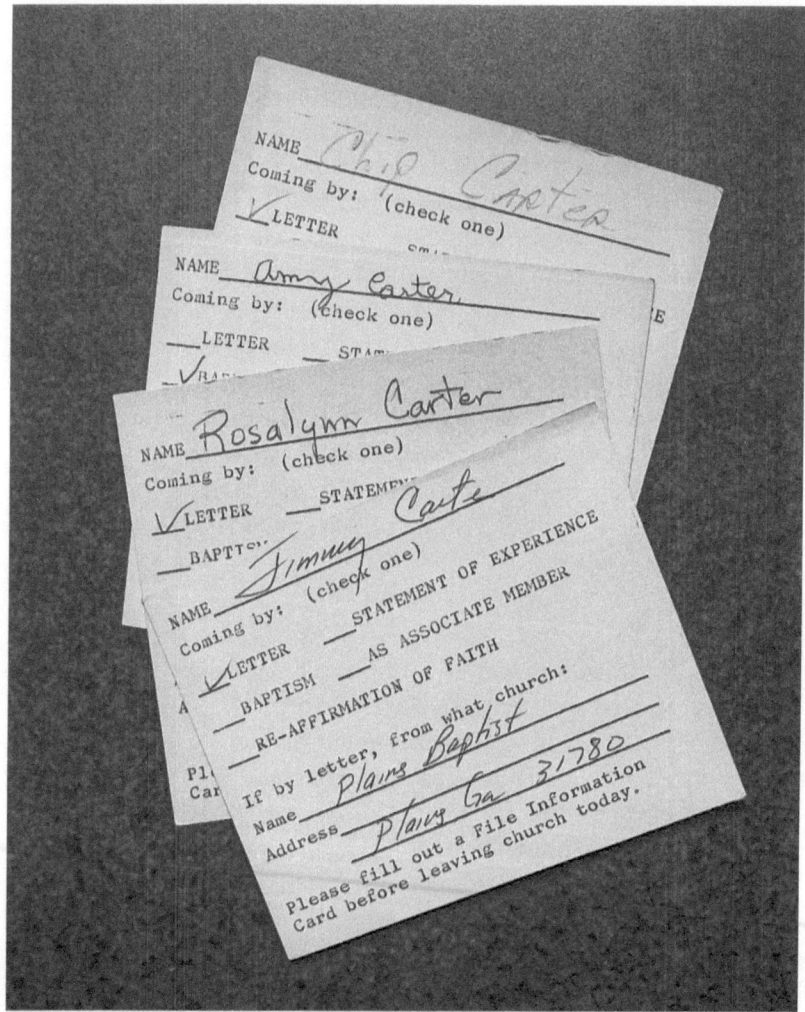

Like all prospective church members, the Carters were asked to fill out and sign small blue cards indicating how they wished to join First Baptist. Jimmy, Rosalynn and their son Chip checked "transfer" from Plains Baptist Church in Georgia. Amy Carter checked "baptism."

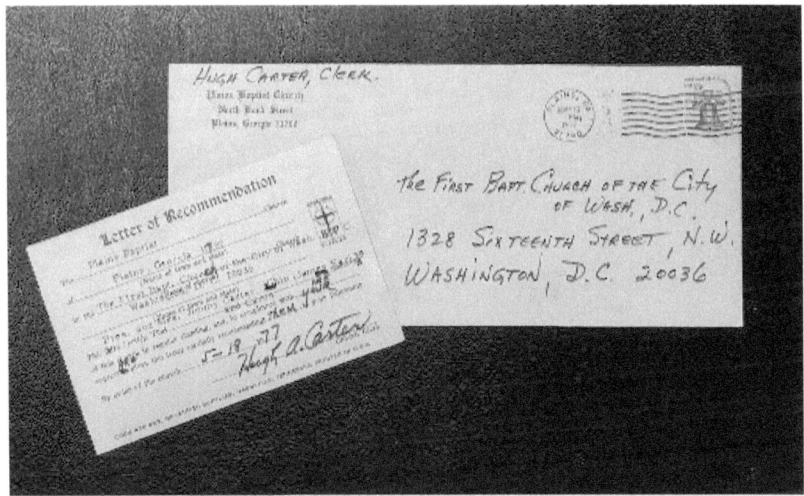

The letter of recommendation from Plains Baptist Church in Georgia, attesting that Jimmy and Rosalynn Carter were members in good standing and "cordially recommending them" to fellowship with First Baptist D.C.

Photos by Tim Pennington-Russell, First Baptist D.C.

THE BAPTISM

A very embarrassed worshiper at Washington's First Baptist Church tried to ask a man sitting on the end of the pew to move over so she could sit down before she realized it was President Carter. She was obligingly shown a seat elsewhere.

Carter was holding the seats yesterday for his wife and his daughter Amy until they could return to their places. Amy was scheduled for baptism. The President had brought Amy's coat along.

WILLIAM F. WILLOUGHBY

WASHINGTON STAR, FEBRUARY 7, 1977

On Sunday, February 6, 1977, the only daughter of Jimmy and Rosalynn Carter stepped into a chest-deep pool of water behind the altar at First Baptist D.C. with the church's senior pastor.

The sanctuary was packed with church members, curious visitors and news reporters, including Janis Johnson of the *Washington Post*, who described the scene:

> Amy Carter was baptized into the Christian faith by full immersion yesterday in front of her mother and father, her nurse, and more than 1,000 fellow worshipers at First Baptist Church.
>
> The red floor-to-ceiling curtains at the front of the gothic-style

sanctuary parted as President Carter's nine-year-old daughter and the church's pastor, the Rev. Dr. Charles A. Trentham, walked slowly into a heated baptismal pool behind the altar.

Amy, wearing a white robe over undergarments, stood with her right side to the congregation, her head just visible. ...

While President Carter sat with his eyes closed in prayer, Dr. Trentham placed his left hand behind Amy's head, raised his right hand and prayed:

"Amy Carter, upon your profession of faith in Christ as your savior and Lord, and in obedience to his command, I baptize you, my sister, in the name of the Father, the Son and the Holy Spirit," Trentham said, before lowering her backward until her head and torso were under water.

President Carter holds Amy's hand as they leave First Baptist D.C. after her baptism on February 6, 1977. *Photo courtesy of the Jimmy Carter Presidential Library*

Johnson's article appeared the next day on the front page of the *Post*'s Metro section under a large photo of the Carters leaving First Baptist and the headline "Amy Carter Baptized Here." A subhead read, "President's Daughter Immersed in Heated Pool."

The only news to Baptists might have been that (1) the baptismal pool was heated and (2) it was an official pool. Baptism is baptism, whether it's done in a river, a pond or a horse tank. Heated water is optional. The crowd size was a little bigger than usual for a baptism, but the public nature of the immersion was a must.

The religion editor of the *Washington Star*, William F. Willoughby, did his best to explain the ritual to his readers:

> Thus, on the third Sunday in the church, the President's daughter publicly professed her faith in Christ, a tradition that goes back to the early 1660s when the Baptists emerged as a sect.
>
> Privately, there was considerable discussion of the baptism being a matter of exploitation for publicity's sake. But anyone aware of the Baptist concept of baptism and its significance could not long entertain the thought. The family and the pastor tried to keep it as low-key as possible, in fact, with cameramen barred.
>
> One of the most frequent questions asked, particularly by Catholics and Episcopalians, who practice infant baptism, is "why wasn't she baptized before her father became President?"
>
> The simplest and most accurate answer is that she did not feel she was ready. She, and not her parents, under Baptist belief, must make the decision.
>
> In the mainstream of Baptist faith, baptism is not permitted until there is clearest evidence, after examination, that the one to be baptized has a solid comprehension of what it means to be saved or born again.

As Willoughby noted, news cameras were not allowed inside First Baptist during the service, but many were waiting outside after Amy's baptism. The cameras captured the young girl, eyes downcast, holding her father's left hand as they walked down the church steps to the waiting motorcade.

The attention might explain the Carters' unexpected abandonment of presidential norms that Sunday afternoon: They went to the opera without telling anyone.

The United Press International was peeved:

> President and Mrs. Carter and newly baptized daughter Amy eluded reporters and slipped away from the White House yesterday for an afternoon performance of Puccini's "Madame Butterfly" at the Kennedy Center.
>
> The pool of White House reporters that normally accompanies

the President discovered he was at the opera only on a tip from a showgoer.

Carter's Sunday-duty assistant press secretary, Pat Bario, said she didn't know he was going until newsmen started asking questions. ...

Reporters finally caught up with Carter as he left the Kennedy Center after the Washington Opera Society production.

A reporter shouted, "You surprised us," and the President replied: "Oh really? It was wonderful."

THE CHURCH

THE BRICKS AND MORTAR

First Baptist comes closest to being like a cathedral for Southern Baptists, whose 36,000 churches generally are not elaborate.

Its expansive balconies and numerous alcoves, separated by cathedral-like columns, make for serious security problems, and the Secret Service was very much in evidence.

It is the same congregation—but not the same church building—that President Harry Truman frequently worshiped in when he was in office. Then it had 1,800 members; now it has 950.

The pastor then was Dr. Edward Hughes Pruden, now pastor emeritus. ...

Because of its elaborate wood carvings surrounding the baptistry, its elegant stained-glass windows and the high tone of its worship services, it often is referred to as "Pruden's Cathedral."

WILLIAM F. WILLOUGHBY

WASHINGTON STAR, JANUARY 24, 1977

As a reporter observed on the Carters' first Sunday in worship at First Baptist D.C. on January 23, 1977, the church's tall columns and soaring ceiling are nothing like the sanctuary of Plains Baptist Church, then the family's church home in Georgia.

Paul Dolinsky, an architect who helped create the Jimmy Carter

National Historical Park in Plains, Georgia, during his 40 years with the National Park Service, described both First Baptist D.C. and Plains Baptist Church as "architecturally well-designed in a Gothic revival style."

"The Plains Baptist Church is an early 20th century rural provincial interpretation of the style, constructed of wood with a clapboard exterior and an asymmetrical facade accented with two towers of different heights," Dolinsky said. "First Baptist D.C. is a more formal Collegiate Gothic style, symmetrical and constructed of stone. A primary difference is the interior. First Baptist D.C. has a processional center aisle focusing on the altar, while Plains Baptist Church has curved pews with side aisles embracing the centrally located pulpit."

The design of the Carters' church home during their four years as First Family was the brainchild of the congregation's 12th pastor, Edward Hughes Pruden. Pruden had studied at the University of Edinburgh and returned to the United States with a Ph.D. and an admiration for the architecture of Anglican and Presbyterian churches in Scotland.

In 1936, shortly after taking charge of the pulpit at First Baptist, Dr. Pruden began lobbying for a new church building. He pointed out that the sanctuary, located on the second floor and accessible by a single staircase, was both a fire hazard and a threat to the security of the church's most prominent attendee, President Harry S. Truman.

Sixteen years would pass before church members approved a new building, the fifth to house the congregation since its founding in 1802.

The congregation's first house of worship was built in record time, especially for Baptists. Between January and September 1802, the tiny congregation raised $225 to purchase a plot of land at 19th and I Streets NW and constructed a 42- by 32-foot brick building for worship.

First Baptist stayed in the heart of D.C.—never far from the White House—from its founding. After more than three decades in the building at 19th and I, the congregation moved to 10th Street NW in 1834. Eleven years later, First Baptist merged with Fourth Baptist and moved into the latter's building on 13th Street.

First Baptist sold the 10th Street building to an empresario from

Baltimore. The National Park Service, which now controls the site, provides this history:

> The Ford's Theatre building was first constructed in 1833 as the First Baptist Church. In 1859, the structure was abandoned as a place of worship. John T. Ford, a theatre entrepreneur from Baltimore, leased the building in 1861. A church board member predicted a dire fate would [be]fall anyone who turned the former house of worship into a theatre. In 1862, Ford renovated the theatre and performances began, setting in motion events to follow that would shake America to its core.

In the 1880s, First Baptist joined industrialists, politicians and socialites gravitating to 16th Street, which led due north from the White House at 1600 Pennsylvania Avenue. In a 2023 book about the "Avenue of Ambitions," John DeFerrari and Douglas Peter Sefton wrote of First Baptist's fourth building: "Dedicated in 1889, the massive brick-over-stone Romanesque Revival church was among the city's grandest, with an amphitheater-like sanctuary that seated 1,300 worshipers. The *Post* called it 'handsome and imposing,' while the *Star* reported that it represented 'the best school of modern architecture.' "

The building, whose campanile, or bell tower, dominated the 16th Street skyline for more than four decades, was well past its prime when Dr. Pruden became pastor. But he had a hell of a time getting a new church built.

For a group that honors free will, Baptists are extraordinarily devoted to committees and procedures, which can starve a project of oxygen. And because Baptists embrace free will, one member can secretly meet with a lender and dissuade investment in a new building, essentially replacing oxygen with poison.

To Dr. Pruden's chagrin, one member did block a loan for the new building. Not once, but twice.

When a third lender was located, the building committee refused to identify the company, fearing more interference from the intermeddler, who resigned and was replaced by a member more amenable to a new building.

Finally, on May 3, 1949, the *Washington Star* reported on plans for a new church building and the congregation's plans to raise $600,000 toward the estimated total cost of $1.25 million. In 2024 dollars, the church members were looking at a capital campaign to raise $19 million toward a total cost of almost $40 million.

After a final service in the old building in 1953, the congregation decamped and moved its services two blocks away to a borrowed auditorium at the D.C. Jewish Community Center.

"Our Sunday School classes met in several buildings over a four-block area, and we referred to this section of 16th Street as our Baptist campus," Dr. Pruden wrote in a later booklet about the construction. "On Sunday mornings, the neighborhood presented a busy scene as people from different buildings came to the Jewish Community Center for worship."

The first worship service in the new sanctuary was held Christmas Day 1955. A little over 21 years later, President Jimmy Carter and his family took seats in a pew a few rows from the pulpit. It was theirs for the next four years.

FROM THE ARCHIVES

During his presidency, Harry S. Truman would occasionally walk north from the White House along 16th Street NW to worship at nearby First Baptist D.C., whose bell tower (center) dominates the skyline in this photo from 1951. The red-brick church, built in 1889, was demolished in 1953. *Photo courtesy of Kiplinger Research Library, DC History Center*

THE PEWS

As we neared the completion of the building in the fall of 1955, we set Christmas Day as a goal for the first service in the new sanctuary. This seemed a reasonable goal if we could just get the pews delivered in time.

DR. EDWARD HUGHES PRUDEN

BUILDING THE HOUSE OF GOD: SOME MEMORIES

Dr. Pruden was right to worry about the pews. More than 150 years earlier, the founding members of First Baptist D.C. had done a great job of buying the land and constructing the first church building in 1802, but the financial effort tapped out the little congregation.

"[I]t was not until 1809 that the building was equipped with pews, which were rented to the congregation to cover expenses," wrote church historian Dorothy Clark Winchcole. (She did not say whether members stood during worship for seven years or came to church with their own chairs.)

A brass plaque now marks the pew where the Carters and their guests worshipped from 1977 to 1981. At time, the sanctuary contained 31 rows of wooden pews that would seat 1,200 people. Getting those seats into the newly completed sanctuary was almost as fraught in 1955 as it was for the earliest congregation. Dr. Pruden told the story to mark the 30th anniversary of the current building:

Just two weeks before Christmas, the pews arrived, brought down from Philadelphia on trucks. They had been made by a Czechoslovakian, who looked upon his work as a work of art and, being anxious to see that the pews were installed correctly, he sent his own team of carpenters with the pews.

The sanctuary of First Baptist D.C. The Carters sat in a pew on the right side, about six or seven rows from the pulpit.
Photo by Tim Pennington-Russell, First Baptist D.C.

When they arrived here, the local carpenters who were already at work in the building raised some kind of jurisdictional labor issue, saying that if the carpenters from Philadelphia came into the building, they would walk out! So we spent all that day having conversations with the labor unions, but to no avail. The loaded trucks turned around and went back to Philadelphia.

We spent all of that week negotiating and finally thought we had it settled, but when the pews arrived the second time, we were confronted by the same problems and spent another day negotiating, but again without success. That afternoon, the trucks, loaded with our pews, returned a second time to Philadelphia. These pews made three trips to Washington before they were ever installed in the building! Ours are the most traveled pews in the United States and perhaps hold some unique place in church history! They were finally installed under hurried circumstances extending into Christmas Eve.

That Christmas Eve several of us were here cleaning up the shavings and dust and getting the room ready for worship the next morning. At two-thirty Christmas morning, the red curtain was hung by a Jewish curtain-maker, who said he did not want us to be disappointed.

You can imagine, then, with what emotions we entered the building Christmas morning to worship God: some walked down the aisles with tears streaming down their faces, and all of us feeling that God guides, God provides, and God brings to fruition.

THE WINDOWS

The announcement of General [Sam] Houston's immersion, a church peri-odical reported, "has excited the wonder and surprise of many who have supposed that he was 'past praying for.' "

SAM HOUSTON ONLINE BIOGRAPHY

SAM HOUSTON STATE UNIVERSITY, 1993

The sanctuary of First Baptist D.C. is lined by 64 tall stained-glass windows, each depicting an event or teaching from the life of Jesus Christ. When the sunlight is at certain angles, the jewel tones of the windows are reflected on the sanctuary's pillars, creating a mosaic of bright colors on gray stone.

Sixteen smaller windows line the sanctuary and depict, on scarlet backgrounds, "Baptist laymen, missionaries, authors, preachers, hymn writers, pioneers, translators and educators," according to a rededication program from November 6, 1988. (Some Baptists did more than one thing.) Way up high, where the walls meet the vaulted ceiling of the sanctuary, are the 16 windows honoring "great Christian leaders from all denominations worldwide," including Saint Francis of Assisi, Martin Luther, John Calvin and David Livingstone.

From his pew a few rows in front of the pulpit, President Carter could look up to the balconies on either side of the sanctuary and see a dozen square windows with backgrounds of cobalt blue. Those windows feature "prominent leaders in world history of the Baptist persuasion," the 1988 program said.

Directly in Carter's line of sight in the south balcony was the window of celebrated scientist George Washington Carver, who knew a thing or two or two hundred about peanuts. Among the other luminaries of Baptist persuasion in the frame are Harry Emerson Fosdick, a liberal Protestant minister; B. H. Carroll, a preacher and founding leader of the Baylor Theological Seminary, which later became Southwestern Baptist Theological Seminary; and Russell H. Conwell, founder of Temple University in Philadelphia.

Also in the frame with Carver: a window dedicated to "The Average Baptist" and donated by the late Charles B. McInnis "in honor of the unnamed Baptists of this Church without whose help this Sanctuary would not have been built."

Above the Average Baptist, and immediately to the left of Carver, is the unlikely Baptist: Sam Houston, two-time president of the Republic of Texas, governor (at different times) of both Tennessee and Texas, later a U.S. senator from Texas, and a man whose best-known spiritual devotion was to a bottle, not Jesus.

Histories published by the eponymous Sam Houston State University and by Baylor University describe Sam Houston as being born into a Presbyterian family, finding much to admire in the Cherokee religion, briefly converting to Catholicism, and eventually occupying a pew in the Baptist Church on E Street in Washington, where he reportedly spent the sermons whittling.

"Late that year [1854], upon hearing a sermon delivered by Baylor President Rufus Burleson, Houston committed his life to Christ," Baylor University recounted in a 2016 blog post on Houston's connections to the Baptist institution. "Wasting no time, Burleson baptized Houston in Independence's Rocky Creek [in Texas]. After being told his sins were washed away, Houston, who led a very colorful life, is said to have quipped, 'God save the fishes.' "

The colorful window honoring Sam Houston was a gift of former U.S. senator and three-term Texas governor Price Daniel Sr. Daniel was serving as director of the Office of Emergency Preparedness under President Lyndon B. Johnson when the stained-glass windows of First Baptist, including his tribute to Sam Houston, were dedicated at services on October 13, 1968.

The sermon at the two services—one at 9:30 a.m., one at 11—were delivered by Dr. George R. Beasley-Murray, principal of Spurgeon's College in London, a Baptist institution founded in 1856 by Charles Spurgeon, whose memorial window at First Baptist D.C. is among the clearly identified Baptists and labeled B-7 in guides to the windows.

The service closed with a prayer of dedication and benediction by the pastor emeritus, Dr. Edward Hughes Pruden, immediately after the congregation joined in the hymn "O Where Are Kings and Empires Now."

THE PASTORS

I have resolved to keep my sermons from being newsworthy.

Dr. Charles A. Trentham
Pastor of First Baptist D.C.

The headline on the full-page article in *People* magazine nailed it: "The First Family Picks a Church and Finds an Unusual Southern Baptist Preacher in the Pulpit."

Tall and handsome, Charles Trentham (pronounced "TREN-um," without the "th") was professionally and personally outside the norm to be the senior pastor of a Southern Baptist church: He was exceptionally progressive on social issues, and he had divorced his first wife while pastor of the First Baptist Church of Knoxville, Tennessee. Members of First Baptist D.C. knew of the divorce, but some were surprised when Trentham arrived in Washington newly wed to a woman from the choir of his Knoxville church.

For most of three years, Trentham made news, not with his sermons, but by being photogenic: The cameras that followed President Carter often captured the pastor with sweeping silver hair and flowing robes greeting the presidential party on the church steps.

In the fall of 1979, Trentham's personal life pushed First Baptist D.C. into the news. He had divorced his second wife and begun socializing with the daughter of a lay leader of the D.C. church. Finding this activity unseemly, a group of deacons moved that Trentham's contract not be renewed when it was up in February 1980. A congregational vote favored the motion, 166 to 140.

"Sunday's emotional two-hour debate focused on the 60-year-old pastor's personal life, including the issue of his two divorces and his relationship with the 28-year-old divorced daughter of a church deacon," the *Washington Star* reported.

The *Washington Post* was more staid in its report of October 29, 1979: "The Carter family was absent from the service and the meeting, held in the church's fellowship hall at 16th and O streets NW. A White House aide said the president 'won't be making any comment' about the matter."

The *Washington Star* quoted at length from a statement issued by Trentham about his divorces, his relationship with the younger woman and "the real cause of his congregation's discontent."

"I want now to lift up the real issue before the façade of personal attacks against me," Trentham said, according to the *Star*. "The issue concerns the point at which moral impacts upon the political. I have been accused of politicizing the pulpit."

The *Star* added: "Trentham said his opponents objected to his statements supporting the Equal Rights Amendment and the SALT II treaty."

However imaginative, the treaty defense didn't persuade sufficient numbers of a congregation that had seen its president, its pastor and the pastor's predilections linked in unsavory news coverage. Trentham was voted out.

———

Unlike Catholics or even many Protestant denominations, such as Methodists, Baptists don't have a hierarchy that maintains a pool of ministers and assigns them to specific churches. Each Baptist church is on its own to recruit, retain and fire leadership, and Baptist churches will often engage an interim pastor while searching for a "permanent" minister—"permanent" being relative among free-will Baptists.

After Trentham's departure, First Baptist D.C. called on a pastor who had retired after 30 years leading Calvary Baptist Church in

Washington, the Reverend Dr. Clarence "Cranny" Cranford, who took up his duties as interim preaching minister at First Baptist D.C. in February 1980. He and President Carter became close.

Dr. Cranford regularly attended Sunday School with the Couples Class, often fielding questions specifically directed to him when Carter was teaching and enduring Carter's teasing when he would duck out of class early to prepare for his sermon. Carter wrote the foreword to a book of sermon illustrations published in 1988 shortly after Dr. Cranford died:

"Among the many bright spots in my life as President of the United States was attending First Baptist Church in Washington with Dr. Clarence Cranford as our pastor. His sermons were always inspirational and entertaining, even enough to keep the attention of Amy and her early teenage friends riveted on the pulpit."

———

Dr. Trentham died in a head-on car collision in Colorado in July 1992. He was the passenger in a car driven by his third wife, who was not the young woman he was seeing when he left First Baptist D.C. Two people in the oncoming car also died, according to news accounts; Trentham's wife was injured but survived.

At the time of his death, Trentham was pastor of the nondenominational Church of the Redeemer in Farragut, Tennessee. Accounts of the car crash in newspapers in Colorado and Tennessee noted prominently that Trentham had been pastor to President Jimmy Carter in Washington, D.C.

The Reverend Dr. Charles A. Threntham with Jimmy and Rosalynn Carter outside First Baptist D.C. *Photo courtesy of the Jimmy Carter Presidential Library.*

FROM THE ARCHIVES

In the foreword to a book of sermons he preached during his long tenure at First Baptist D.C., the Reverend Dr. Edward Hughes Pruden described the unique challenge of being a pastor in Washington, D.C., and the unique nature of First Baptist, which, at the time, was affiliated with both the American and Southern Baptist conventions.

These sermons have been preached to one of the most interesting congregations imaginable. Sitting before me each Sunday are people from practically every state in the Union, also representatives of many foreign countries, and individuals with a variety of denominational affiliations.

The congregation is never the same on any two Sundays; and, as a fellow pastor expressed it, "preaching in Washington is like trying to evangelize a parade."

Not only are the Government employees coming and going constantly, many of them being transferred to other cities just when we are beginning to depend on them within our church family, but every Sunday there are numerous visitors to the Capital City. One does not have to move to another city in order to acquire a new congregation. In Washington, the new congregation comes to the minister. ...

I sincerely trust that these sermons will serve to interpret our Baptist people to one another, for that is one of the services we have seriously undertaken to render here in the nation's Capital.

Our church is affiliated with both of our national Baptist conventions, and it has succeeded in molding Baptists from the North, the South, the East, and the West into one harmonious spiritual family. Its members have discovered within the fellowship of our church that whatever differences they may have recognized before coming to Washington are inconsequential when compared with the truly significant ideals they hold in common.

Many of them have been frankly surprised to discover that some of the rumors they had heard regarding one another were wholly unfounded. We are seeking also to carry this same spirit over into a larger realm, and to create not only a national but also an international fellowship made up of the wide variety of nationalities which are represented in the Capital City.

THE DENOMINATION

I don't accept any domination of my life by the Baptist Church, none. Every Baptist church is individual and autonomous. We don't accept domination of our church from the Southern Baptist Convention. The reason the Baptist Church was formed in this country was because of our belief in absolute and total separation of church and state.

JIMMY CARTER
DEMOCRATIC PRESIDENTIAL NOMINEE
PLAYBOY, NOVEMBER 1976

One reason Jimmy Carter gave for joining First Baptist D.C. was its affiliation with the Southern Baptist Convention, the organization formed in 1845 when U.S. Baptists, following their brethren among the Presbyterians and Methodists, split on North-South lines in disagreement over enslavement.

At the time Carter joined, First Baptist D.C. was also affiliated with the American Baptist Convention—the northern counterpart to the Southern Baptists. The church had long embraced progressive policies more in line with American Baptists, creating a mixed-gender Sunday School class in the 1940s and counting Black members in its fellowship from its founding.

Affiliation with any Baptist organization—Southern, Northern or

American—didn't mean much beyond sharing expenses for developing and printing Sunday School curricula, funding seminaries and collectively supporting domestic and foreign missionaries. Individual Baptist churches own their land and buildings, set their own governance policies and hire or fire their own pastors.

In the 1970s, Southern Baptists were as ubiquitous as Southern Democrats. If you were a Baptist, you were most likely affiliated with a Southern Baptist church. If you were a politician in the South, you were almost certainly a Democrat. Carter, a progressive, became governor of Georgia in 1971, the same year segregationist George Wallace was elected to his second term as governor of Alabama. They were both Democrats.

When Carter was elected president in 1976, the Southern Baptist Convention was still a big tent. Convention delegates, known as messengers, elected a progressive friend of Carter's, Jimmy R. Allen, as president. Carter welcomed a group of about 75 members of the Southern Baptist Brotherhood Commission to the White House Rose Garden in June 1977.

But the conservative drift of the Southern Baptists began during Carter's presidency. The annual report for the group's 1977 meeting included a summary of world events from the Foreign Missons Board with this note about 1976: "In the United States, attention focused on the Bicentennial celebrations and on the Presidential election, with a Baptist deacon Jimmy Carter, helping the South to 'rise again.' "

By the time Carter left office, the so-called "conservative resurgence" had pushed the Southern Baptist Convention far to the right. The move coincided with the conservative movement that helped Ronald Reagan defeat Carter in 1980 and the rise of quasi-religious organizations such as the Moral Majority.

On his first Sunday at First Baptist D.C. after losing the election, Carter wrote in his diary: "I enjoyed teaching the Sunday school class. The visiting preacher, Dr. [Claude] Broach, spoke very bluntly about the Moral Majority and its threat as ayatollahs of religion in our country."

Carter left office in January 1981, joined Maranatha Baptist Church in Plains, Georgia, and resumed teaching Sunday School there. The Southern Baptist Convention kept lurching farther and farther to the right. In response, moderate Baptists threatened in 1990 to withhold contributions to the organization in what a headline in the *Washington Post* called a "collection plate revolt." Reporter Gus Niebuhr summarized the issue for the *Wall Street Journal*:

"Since fundamentalists took control of the denomination in 1979, moderates have charged that they have not been given a fair voice in denomination affairs. Those who don't hold certain conservative political and religious views—such as favoring school prayer, strictly opposing abortion, upholding a literal interpretation of the Bible—are penalized. They have been shut out of leadership positions, and some have even been fired."

The hard right turn continued until 2000 when, in the view of many Baptists, the organization of their upbringing drove right into a ditch. (In more recent developments, the Southern Baptists picked up shovels and started digging a deeper ditch, but that's a story for someone else's book.) Carter was among those who refused to follow.

At issue in 2000 was the vote by messengers to the annual meeting of the Southern Baptist Convention to adopt the "Baptist Faith & Message" that, to many, did not mesh with the very, very broad tent that Jesus built. Among the pieces of the message:

Man is the special creation of God, made in His own image. He created them male and female as the crowning work of His creation. The gift of gender is thus part of the goodness of God's creation.

While both men and women are gifted for service in the church, the office of pastor/elder/overseer is limited to men as qualified by Scripture.

In the spirit of Christ, Christians should oppose racism, every form of greed, selfishness, and vice, and all forms of sexual immorality, including adultery, homosexuality, and pornography.

Marriage is the uniting of one man and one woman in covenant commitment for a lifetime.

A wife is to submit herself graciously to the servant leadership of her husband even as the church willingly submits to the headship of Christ. She, being in the image of God as is her husband and thus equal to him, has the God-given responsibility to respect her husband and to serve as his helper in managing the household and nurturing the next generation.

In October 2000, Jimmy Carter publicly announced that he was parting ways with the Southern Baptist Convention. He shared a "personal reflection" with like-minded Baptists, including the now-defunct Texas Baptists Committed, which published his statement. It reads in part:

To My Fellow Baptists,

Like millions of other Baptists, I have been deeply distressed by the unpleasant and counterproductive divisions within our denomination. In November 1997 and March 1998, I invited two dozen Baptist leaders to The Carter Center, in an attempt to overcome differences that were impeding our common mission "to bring about a spiritual awakening in our nation and around the world."

I had never been involved in the political struggle for control of the SBC, and have no desire to do so. My hope was that, as a traditional Baptist layman, I could find some channel through which I could help fulfill our Christian commitments. But since that brief interlude of apparent harmony, I have been disappointed and feel excluded by the adoption of policies and an increasingly rigid SBC creed, including some provisions that violate the basic premises of my Christian faith. I have finally decided that, after 65 years, I can no longer be associated with the Southern Baptist Convention.

What am I to do? I'll certainly continue in my role as a deacon and Sunday School teacher at Maranatha Baptist Church and support sending half our mission contribution to the Cooperative Baptist Fellowship. In addition to our fellow church members, Rosalynn and I have been trying to identify other traditional Baptists who share such beliefs as separation of church and state, servanthood of pastors, priesthood of believers, a free religious press, and equality of women. ...

As Georgia Baptists, we are quite concerned by the effort of SBC leaders to impose their newly adopted creed on our state convention. Our prayer is that we can avoid this divisive action, and adhere to the traditional beliefs that, for generations, have sustained our ancestors and us in a spirit of unity and cooperation.

At about the same time that Carter quit the Southern Baptist Convention, First Baptist D.C. dropped its affiliation with the group.

THE STEEPLE

THE STEEPLE

There is no steeple on the First Baptist Church of Washington, D.C.

Dr. Edward Hughes Pruden's original plans—published in an architect's rendering in the *Washington Post* and *Washington Star* in May 1949—included a tall spire. President Harry Truman, who had seen the drawing in the *Post*, told Dr. Pruden the spire was too small.

"[Truman] said that he was somewhat of an amateur architect, having made something of a study of cathedrals he had seen in Europe, and that his only disagreement with our architect was regarding the size of the steeple over the main entrance," Dr. Pruden wrote later. "He thought it was not in keeping with the massive size of the edifice itself."

But when construction got underway in 1953, the congregation had given all it could financially. Plans changed. There would be no steeple, nor would there be an impressive organ to fill the space left for pipes in a sanctuary built for the sound.

A later effort to erect the steeple found that even the supporting infrastructure had been abandoned in the 1950s. First Baptist would remain a squat, truncated building. But the space—and vision—for a magnificent organ was still alive.

In 2011, another doctoral graduate of the University of Edinburgh —albeit one with less ambitious architectural leanings than Dr. Pruden—led a campaign to raise $2 million for the design, purchase and installation of a 6,000-pipe organ. Thanks largely to the fundraising efforts of Dr. Dennis Lambert, the music envisioned by Dr. Pruden more than 60 years earlier began to fill the sanctuary in 2013.

The view of a spire against the sky can draw eyes toward heaven. Music can carry the heart and soul.

FROM THE ARCHIVES

Dr. Pruden envisioned a soaring spire for the building that First Baptist D.C. undertook in 1953. He shared the artist's rendering of the steepled structure with both Washington newspapers and on the cover of his 1951 book.

The price tag for the new building was as high as the steeple, and the embellishment was scrapped.

Photos by Tim Pennington-Russell, First Baptist D.C.

THE PEOPLE

THE PREDECESSORS

President Johnson gave the surprised congregation of First Baptist Church a double attraction Sunday by bringing along evangelist Billy Graham. ... After the hour-long 11 a.m. service, the Johnsons and Dr. Graham gathered with the congregation in a basement meeting room for handshaking and refreshments—orange punch and cookies.

United Press International

Washington Post, September 12, 1966

For a congregation that was founded in 1802, First Baptist can count only a handful of close encounters with U.S. presidents.

Thomas Jefferson was president when First Baptist was formed, and he penned a letter to the church's first pastor, Obadiah B. Brown, in October 1808, apparently responding to a message of appreciation for Jefferson's role in establishing the separation of church and state in the still-new United States. Jefferson demurred, saying the credit should be shared: "In our early struggles for liberty, religious freedom could not fail to become a primary object. All men felt the right, and a just animation to obtain it was excited in all. I was one only among the many who befriended its establishment and am entitled but in common with others to a portion of that approbation which follows the fulfilment of a duty."

More than 100 years later, President Warren G. Harding was impressed by the preaching of Henry Allan Tupper, the church's ninth pastor (1918 to 1923) who was said to be "magnetic in personality, endowed with a great sense of humor and a gifted orator."

Harding came frequently enough to the church, in its first building at 16th and O streets, that a pew was reserved for him. (Tupper's daughter, Katherine, a widow, would later marry a widower and rising Army officer, George C. Marshall.)

During Tupper's tenure, First Baptist celebrated its 120th anniversary, and the speakers included William Jennings Bryan, a lawyer and three-time presidential nominee. Ten years later, President Herbert Hoover dispatched a staffer to the church's 130th anniversary celebration.

"The message from the President was read by Walter H. Newton, one of his secretaries, who in a brief address of felicitation spoke of the influence of Baptist leaders in the Nation since the founding of the Republic," a newspaper reported. Hoover's message concluded: "First Baptist has earned a place of lasting affection and influence which I gladly recognize and warmly admire."

When the church hit its 150th anniversary in 1952, President Harry S. Truman was a regular enough attendee that he could get personal in his message to the congregation: "May I, in extending hearty felicitations and warmest personal greetings, express the hope that our church will go from strength to strength thru all the generations ahead."

Truman was the last sitting president to attend services in the 1889-era building. By the time Lyndon Johnson popped by with Billy Graham for worship and orange punch in 1966, First Baptist had been in its new building for almost 11 years. (Graham was a Baptist; Johnson worshipped at National City Christian Church, a few blocks east of First Baptist.)

Jimmy Carter was governor of Georgia when Truman died in 1972 and Johnson in 1973. Carter never met either man, although he spoke admiringly of each and even worked LBJ into a Sunday School lesson on June 25, 1978—less than 15 hours after returning from a two-day tour of Texas that mixed presidential activities with political.

At 10 a.m. that Sunday, Carter launched into a lesson from Genesis, using the story of Joseph and his brothers to teach a lesson of humanity and redemption. He emphasized that no one has to be defined by bad decisions, whether those are boasting, selling a brother into slavery or prolonging a war. Supplementing the biblical text, Carter brought up the legacy of President Johnson:

> Since I've been in the White House, I've read a lot of biographies, long and short, about my predecessors there. I could go back down the list of presidents, some of whom are condemned ferociously, some of whom [are] looked on as heroes. ... Some of them are condemned in retrospect because of one incident in their lives as president, over which they had not too much control.
>
> I just came back from Texas. Lyndon Johnson comes to my mind. I don't think there was ever a president who worked harder or who had a greater, more generous heart or who cared more and did more for people who were persecuted and deprived and who felt the stigma and the punishment of racial hatred and prejudice and discrimination.
>
> But when you think about Lyndon Johnson now, you don't think about freedom. You don't think about an end to discrimination. [You] don't think about voting rights acts nearly so much as you think about the Vietnam War. But Johnson was always trying to do things to make a better community, better cities, better highways, better life for people.
>
> And still, he's not one of those presidents, at least yet, who's recognized as big-hearted, great-hearted, concerned about others.

In January 2016, members of the Johnson family traveled to Atlanta to present Carter with the LBJ Liberty & Justice for All Award "in recognition of his leadership in public service and his tireless efforts toward peace and human rights."

Carter is quoted as returning the compliment: "It is a great personal honor to be given the Liberty & Justice for All Award in the name of Lyndon Johnson, a man who helped shape my life and for whom I have the greatest admiration and appreciation."

For Truman, Carter expressed a special affinity in a 1991 oral history interview conducted by a National Park Service historian:

> I thought he was the greatest president of this century. He was always the one that I mentioned when I was asked that question,

never anyone else. I thought about him often when I was in the White House.

He was involved deeply in many of the issues that I had to address, ... but I felt that he was down-to-earth. He was honest. He told the truth even when it was painful. He didn't try to shift blame for disappointments or failures to other people. He was courageous, and he never ducked an important issue because it might cost him a few points in the public opinion poll.

Also, I felt kind of a kinship with him. We both came from a kind of community that was similar in some ways, and we went back home after the election and the service in the White House.

Carter didn't mention that he had also shared a church with Truman in the congregation of First Baptist D.C.

THE MULTITUDES

Somehow, Carter watchers from Washington to the Far West find out the President's schedule ... and on the days he is expected at church, spectators swarm into First Baptist in such throngs that members now have to arrive early a half-hour or more to find a seat.

JANIS JOHNSON

WASHINGTON POST, JUNE 17, 1977

Less than three weeks after the Carters became members of First Baptist, the church's social committee published a plaintive plea in the church newsletter: "The Visitors' Coffee regularly held in the parlor on all but the second Sundays of the month now require certain limitations which we request our congregation to observe. Our many visitors, some 200 each week, present a problem for the Visitors' Coffee. ... [W]e request that members refrain from just 'dropping by' for a cup of coffee as such."

Eight months later, the hospitality team repeated the request that members lay off the caffeine with one change: The number of visitors had jumped to 300 each week.

The Carters' arrival and regular attendance—at least 26 Sundays in just the first year, 1977—drew crowds that stretched the resources of the volunteers who get things done in a church. A staff of nine people—including two pastors, the music minister, a secretary and a maintenance engineer—tended to the business of church for a congregation of about 1,000 people (down from a peak of 2,000 in the 1950s). The rest of the work fell to members who set aside their day jobs on Sundays to teach Sunday School, serve as ushers and welcome guests—a lot of guests.

Rosalynn and Jimmy Carter leave First Baptist D.C. as ropes hold back spectators who came to see the First Family. President Carter attended services at the church at least 75 times during his 48 months in office. *Photo courtesy of the Jimmy Carter Presidential Library*

The welcome was warm and appreciated. An early visitor gave the senior pastor permission to publish his letter in the *First Baptist Church News*, and it appeared January 17, 1978:

As a young person who recently moved to the Washington area, I had the pleasure of being a visitor in your church several weeks ago. At the outset I must admit my motives were mixed, as my visiting brother wanted a chance to see President Carter as well. With some reluctance we went to the President's Sunday School class and the morning service. ...

I always thought that having the President of the United States worship in your church would create an unbearable stream of tourists, cameras, and non-worshiping visitors through the aisles.

While I'm sure there are special problems in that respect, from all appearances you have not only provided an atmosphere where the President himself can worship in a normal church setting, but have a congregation which demonstrates warmth and love through the spirit of Christ.

I was personally thankful to see President Carter committed to providing an example of worship for our nation, and that he worships in a church where a visitor leaves with more than just a glimpse of our national leader and his wife.

A glimpse—and, maybe, a handshake—was all that visitors would get from President Carter. In early May 1978, a pharmacist from northwestern Alabama mailed his Sunday bulletin back to First Baptist with a heartfelt exclamation (emphasis on exclamation) of the surprise he got on his first trip to Washington, D.C.:

Words cannot express the joy I found in worship and fellowship with you yesterday. Your hospitality was overwhelming! And I was totally ignorant that our president would be there! What a joy to worship with him, experiencing the same sights and sounds of worship!

I could hardly believe it—and what is even worse, my pastor and the men of my [Sunday School] class are giving me that "You're pulling my leg" smile when I tell them I had the pleasure of shaking hands with our president and worshipping with him.

The pharmacist asked politely if someone at First Baptist could get President Carter's autograph on the bulletin. "I fear it would get lost in the maze of White House mail," he wrote.

Associate Pastor Charles R. Sanks Jr. responded respectfully 10 days later: "I know you will understand how we try to provide a setting for the President and his family to enjoy Bible study and worship among fellow Christians as peers. In order to have their experience as nearly 'normal' as possible, we do not pass on to the President gifts or requests for autographs and the like. We adhere so much to that, that I myself do not have an autograph, even though I am with him regularly. ... Thank you for your support and interest in our Christian witness."

The Christian witness of President Carter at First Baptist

impressed a faculty member of a small Baptist institution in Liberty, Missouri. More than 45 years after he escorted a dozen students from William Jewell College to Washington, D.C., Jerry B. Cain spoke reverentially of the impact on his students of being in the church's Couples Class for Bible study led by Jimmy Carter.

"They got to see the President of the United States up close," Cain said. "It was in church. It wasn't a press conference or a campaign rally. It was a Sunday School class.

"I didn't sense it being a couples' class. I sensed it as a leadership class. It was a good experience, not because of the content but the modeling, that the leaders of our nation went to Sunday School and taught Sunday School."

THE PRESIDENTIAL PARTY

What are you going to do when the President of the United States puts the arm on you? We joined the church.

JOHN C. WHITE

CHAIRMAN OF THE DEMOCRATIC NATIONAL COMMITTEE

AT THE FIRST BAPTIST D.C. ANNIVERSARY BANQUET, APRIL 26, 1978

The newcomers who started appearing in the congregation of First Baptist D.C. in 1977 weren't all onetime visitors. Practiced at packing pews, the Carters brought their share of invited family and friends. Those traveling in the Sunday morning motorcade were named, then collectively referred to as the "Presidential party" in the presidential daily diary.

Among the Carters' more frequent guests were members of the family, including the President's mother, Miss Lillian, and mother-in-law, Allie Smith. A cousin made an appearance, as did an elementary school classmate from Plains and a roommate of Carter's from the Naval Academy. Amy's guests in the Carters' reserved pew included, on one Sunday, then 12-year-old Mika Brzezinski, future MSNBC host and the daughter of Carter's National Security Advisor.

Others from the Carters' orbit went on to join First Baptist, among them Amy's nanny, Mary Prince Fitzpatrick; Attorney General Griffin Bell and his wife; and John C. White, who had resigned his elected post as Texas Commissioner of Agriculture to join the Carter administration.

"In 1977, President Jimmy Carter asked Mr. White to serve as his Deputy Secretary of Agriculture," a biography reads. "His first responsibilities were not easy. Among them was dealing with thousands of farmers, who drove tractors to Washington and demonstrated on the Mall calling for new farm policies."

In December 1977, Carter asked White to be chairman of the Democratic National Committee. White agreed. Then the President had another request, as White recounted in a speech at the 176th anniversary dinner of First Baptist D.C.:

> With great good humor White told how he became a member of First Baptist Church. He was in church with the President when Carter said to him, "John, have you joined a church?"
>
> "No, but we are thinking about it."
>
> "Why don't you join this church?" Carter continued.
>
> "Nellie and I are thinking about it."
>
> "Why don't you join this church today?"
>
> White then said, "What are you going to do when the President of the United States puts the arm on you? We joined the church."

White stayed in Washington after his term as DNC chairman ended in February 1981, working as a consultant to corporations and Democrats. After his death at age 70, the Texas State Historical Association documented the remarkable tributes to his life:

"White died in Washington, D.C., on January 20, 1995. His funeral was the first to be held in the Rotunda of the Texas State Capitol, and Republican George W. Bush was governor. ...

"White's bi-partisanship was best reflected in his two funeral services—a funeral and graveside burial in Austin on January 27, 1995, and a later memorial service at the First Baptist Church of Washington, D.C., on January 31, 1995. Democratic presidential candidate the Rev. Jesse Jackson (whom White helped advise during his 1988 presidential campaign) conducted the funeral and graveside service in Austin."

At the memorial service at First Baptist D.C., the eulogists included Bob Dole, the Republican senator from Kansas, and Robert Strauss, a former chairman of the Democratic National Committee. The cover of the printed program for the service is a photo of White wielding a large gavel at a lectern at the Democratic National Convention.

On the back of the program are nine quotations from White, covering his boyhood on a Texas cotton farm to his thoughts about the upcoming 1996 presidential election. About Washington, D.C., he said, "The way I see Washington, it's not so much Democrats and Republicans, but real people and bleeps, and you find 'em on both sides."

THE PRESS

Dr. [Charles] Trentham announced that he would like to hire a professional news person for one day a week since our church is in the news every time the President is at church. Caspar Nannes has indicated that he could give us his time one day a week for $150 a month. [It was] moved that the Diaconate go on record as favoring such employment of Mr. Nannes. Motion was seconded and carried.

MEETING MINUTES
FIRST BAPTIST D.C. DIACONATE, FEBRUARY 2, 1977

When reporters leave journalism to go into public relations or public affairs or communications, the colleagues left behind often deride the move as "going to the dark side." (Quoting one of my own earliest malapropisms as a spokesperson, "That's horse hockey.")

When the senior pastor of First Baptist D.C. suggested hiring Caspar Nannes to handle publicity around the Carters' attendance, the longtime journalist had already threaded an unlikely path to the unfairly maligned dark arts. He was highly educated—holding a Ph.D. from the University of Pennsylvania—and had moved from being the tennis editor for the *Washington Star* to being religion editor. He won awards in both editorial roles—true love, I say.

The time commitment and compensation Nannes took on at First

Baptist—one day a week for $150 a month—seems unrealistic even by 1977 standards. But unlike many publicity directors, Nannes didn't have to exert much effort to get reporters to cover his client. Reporters came with the territory: the small pool of White House correspondents who traveled everywhere with the president and the religion writers whose beats included churches.

Carter and his aides had a contentious relationship with the White House press corps, but they had no say over the reporters who accompanied him to church. The press pool, composed of wire service reporters and a few representatives of print and broadcast media, was assigned by the White House Correspondents Association, the same group whose annual dinners evolved, or devolved, in the 1990s to be covered—and attended—like the Academy Awards.

President Carter speaks with reporters on the front steps of First Baptist D.C. on November 20, 1977, after an early morning prayer service for peace in the Middle East. Carter skipped Sunday School and worship to return to the White House and watch the television broadcast of Egyptian President Anwar Sadat's address to the Israeli Knesset. *Photo courtesy of the Jimmy Carter Presidential Library*

The WHCA dinners offer presidents the opportunity to poke some fun at the press and themselves; indeed, Carter got laughs from the assembled media and guests at least 20 times during his 23 minutes of remarks at the dinner Saturday, April 30, 1977. The press association gave the President a silver platter; he reciprocated with a mic drop before mic drops were even a thing:

"In closing, let me say that Rosalynn and I appreciate very much the silver centerpiece, and I would also like to express my deep thanks to you for—I would like to express my appreciation to the White House correspondents for … [*laughter*] the sense of gratitude that I have for …[*laughter*]" He never finished the sentence.

One year later, Carter didn't try to joke about his feelings for the press corps, writing in his diary April 25, 1978: Press secretary Jody Powell "[i]s begging me to speak to the White House Correspondents' banquet. My preference is not to do so. They are completely irresponsible and unnecessarily abusive. I see no reason for us to accommodate them every time they want me to provide entertainment for a half hour."

Carter held firm, writing on April 29: "Jody took my place and let them know basically how we feel about them, and other staff members who were there say I didn't miss anything. We didn't see any aftereffects from my absence."

The tiff over the annual dinner didn't affect the coverage arranged by the WHCA, and the press pool continued to accompany President Carter to church and Sunday School. Associate teacher Ed Sonnenschein found the reporters' presence an added stress in an already unsettling situation:

"I never anticipated that when I agreed to be associate teacher that when [regular teacher] Fred Gregg was out of town, I would be teaching to the President of the United States," said Sonnenschein, who worked as an architect. "I'm not a professional speaker, I'm not a theologian. I'm just a Christian man who volunteers for things.

"When Fred was out of town, when Carter was here, it was kind of intimidating. Facing Jimmy and Rosalynn Carter in their seats in the center of the balcony was one thing; the reporters were another.

"First row on the left was press with their steno pads—this was before smart phones," Sonnenschein said. "They were waiting for something to go wrong."

Sonnenschein needn't have worried: The pool reporters weren't there to catch misspoken Scriptures; they were there in case news broke out, such as the President welcoming a former Soviet detainee to class or describing how he spoke of his Baptist faith to the Buddhist leader of South Korea. (Keep reading: you'll get to those stories.)

Separate from the press pool were the journalists for whom religion was a beat; they covered Carter's participation in more churchy events such as Amy's baptism, the influx of visitors at First Baptist D.C. and the ouster of the senior pastor.

When Carter was elected in 1976, Washington had two daily newspapers: the *Washington Post* and the *Washington Star*. Both had religion editors—Marjorie Hyer for the *Post* and William F. Willoughby at the *Star*. The *Post* also had a new, young reporter on the religion beat, Janis Johnson, who wrote the following in a blog post in September 2023:

> Back then, there were two varieties of religion writers, and in the late 1960s and early 1970s the way news media covered religion went through a remarkable transition. Religion writers often were tolerated as a necessity, though not taken seriously as journalism professionals by many of their peers.
>
> Nonetheless as capable writers and reporters, the traditional religion writers tended to concentrate on summaries of Sunday sermons, weekly calendars of events for churches and synagogues and occasional spiritual insights of their own in religion page essays.
>
> The other lot were people like me—general assignment reporters who covered religion news and features just as we would education, politics, the courts or local government. We were usually younger, fresh out of the socially and politically formative 1960s and starting our careers (and religion writing, along with obits, was at the bottom rung of the upward journalism ladder).
>
> You couldn't charge us with being preachy or defending our beliefs in print; we were simply professionally hungry for a good story that would soon graduate us into another more "legitimate" beat.

Johnson was assigned to cover Carter and First Baptist D.C. when he joined the church. She came away with some distinct memories of that Sunday in January 1977.

As the Carters arrived at the church, she said, "It was snowing. It was freezing cold. All of the camera people and news people were crowded on the front steps. The cameramen kept stepping on my toes."

Later, after the service, "We went downstairs into what would be the reception hall, and the President was just walking around, talking to people like he was anyone else."

"What I remember most," Johnson wrote on her blog, "is the consistency of his faith – it was organic and there was nothing false or contrived about it. … Journalists and their editors tend to be skeptics, and with such a devout president in the White House, the religious practice that was normal for him often became a front- or city-page subject of media curiosity."

At Washington's other daily newspaper, the *Star*, Willoughby waxed eloquent about President Carter and his church, writing both news stories and a weekly column on religion. Willoughby had succeeded Caspar Nannes as the *Star's* religion editor after Nannes left the paper in 1968 for freelance gigs.

During the 22 months that Nannes worked with First Baptist, he wrote profiles of church leaders—clerical and lay—for the church newsletter and documented Carters' time at First Baptist for publication in the newsletters of the church and the DC Baptist Convention, and, occasionally, in the Baptist Press, a newswire. After Nannes died in late November 1978, an unattributed appreciation appeared in the *First Baptist Church News*:

"For those of our congregation who knew Dr. Caspar Nannes there is a sense of great personal loss and for others of our fellowship there is the loss of a staff member who contributed to our lives far out of proportion to the two short years of his gifts among us. …

"Dr. Nannes was invaluable to our church at the time of its coming into prominence and public attention when President Carter and his family united with our fellowship. He guided our news releases, interviews and position statements with the skill of a wise newsman."

FROM THE ARCHIVES

The First Family on the front steps of First Baptist D.C. *Photo courtesy of the Jimmy Carter Presidential Library*

The Photographs

The small number of official photos of Jimmy Carter at First Baptist D.C. isn't the fault of this author or the White House staff photographers who travel in every presidential entourage. It is the former president's fault: He hated having his picture taken.

"We had to work for every shot," former White House photographer Bill Fitz-Patrick said in an interview in October 2023.

Photographers have been part of the official White House staff since the administration of John F. Kennedy, tasked with capturing images of the president for history—from the routine meet-and-greets with foreign leaders to the unexpected images that capture a president's candid reaction: Think of the photo of an aide whispering the news of September 11 to President George W. Bush.

Carter would have no part of candid photos, Fitz-Patrick said. "We were starting to get frustrated. I told him once that his presidential library would have nothing but handshake photos."

Carter eventually loosened up—a bit—but not at church. Fitz-Patrick said he accompanied the President to First Baptist a few times but deliberately kept his finger off the shutter button out of respect for other worshippers.

The biggest batch of photos of Carter at First Baptist contains the standard staged images that are routine at White House receptions and banquets. In a dozen or more negatives from the Couples Class banquet in October 1977, Jimmy and Rosalynn Carter are pictured posing with the long tables of seated class members. The class members are in the forefront and, way down at the end of each table, you can just make out the President and First Lady of the United States.

THE GUARDIANS

Mildred New stood at the rear of the First Baptist Church the other day and made a wish for the church's newest members, President Carter and his family. "I hope," Mrs. New began, a trace of a Southern accent in her voice, "this is the one place they can come where they don't have to be the Presidential family, just people."

KENNETH A. BRIGGS

NEW YORK TIMES, JANUARY 30, 1977

Going to church with President Jimmy Carter in Washington, D.C., was surprisingly easy: There were no metal detectors or bag searches at the entrance and no uniformed law enforcement in the sanctuary.

But visitors and church members alike had to deal with two formidable organizations determined to safeguard, respectively, the physicality and the spirituality of the President of the United States: the U.S. Secret Service and the unarmed but equally protective ushers and congregants of First Baptist D.C.

Anyone approaching the church beginning in January 1977 through January 1981 could see the Secret Service snipers on the rooftops of neighboring buildings on 16th Street. "Unsettling" and "eerie," members said of the sight. Less obtrusive were the agents in suits and ties, stationed around the sanctuary during Carter's

Sunday School class in the balcony and, later, the worship service. Then-usher Richard Turner recalled that one agent, about the same height and build as Carter and with similar hair, would always sit near the President's pew as a decoy.

Other official protective measures took place behind the scenes. Dr. Clarence "Cranny" Cranford, the interim preaching minister at First Baptist D.C. in 1980, described the preparations for a magazine of the American Baptist Convention:

"The church staff always knew in advance when the president was coming. No meeting could be held in the sanctuary after noon on Friday for security reasons, if the Carters were coming the following Sunday.

"Manhole covers were sealed within a certain distance of the church and agents secured the building, rifling hymnbooks for envelope bombs, and using police dogs to sniff-out any explosives in every pew and room of the church."

The main security-related inconvenience for worshippers came at the end of the Sunday service, when the congregation was asked to stay seated to allow the presidential party to leave. Those in the pews could meditate; the ushers got busy.

"[O]nce the service is over and things get moving, there's no getting out of line," usher Doug Porter wrote in his diary. "All kinds of things start happening and it's almost an invisible process. Secret Service appear from nowhere, it seems; the members of the press get up and start out; you hear motorcycles start up outside. News and television cameras are bunched up outside trying to get one more shot, [and] police from the Executive [Protective] Agency and D.C. are swarming."

The pastors would leave the sanctuary with President Carter and members of his party.

"Before the service, the Secret Service would choose which door he was to go out and tell only the ministers, who escorted the president to the curb," Cranford recalled. "When [President] Reagan was shot [in March 1981], you know, it made me think: Any Sunday the president came to church when I was there, if anybody had tried to shoot him, I would have been in the middle."

THE LAYING ON OF HANDS

[Diaconate Chairman William McBeath] reported a review had been made of the practices followed in instances of demonstrations. The policy currently in effect was reiterated—we will seek to stop demonstrators that are disrupting our services and it would be a rare case when it would be appropriate for us to ask our ushers to use force in the eviction of demonstrators.

MEETING MINUTES
FIRST BAPTIST D.C. DIACONATE, JULY 11, 1979

Ushers are typically the friendly church members who greet congregants at the front door, offering a bulletin of the morning service and helping newcomers find seats. But President Carter's presence in worship at First Baptist D.C. from 1977 to 1981 required some atypical assignments for the ushers.

"President and Mrs. Carter were in church today," usher Doug Porter wrote in his diary October 14, 1979. "A Street Person strolled all the way down front and started into the President's pew, but [an usher] who was right behind her offered her his arm and escorted her to a place further on down."

Not all intruders were as compliant with the instructions of ushers. An influx of anti-nuke protesters prompted the deacons of First Baptist to publish "Policies for Demonstrations," meant to provide ushers and other church personnel with guidance for dealing politely and non-violently with demonstrators. Among the provisions:

- No demonstration disrupting the convened congregation will be tolerated.
- Demonstrators will be approached by the ushers and invited to leave and then be escorted out of the facilities.
- If the demonstrators refuse to go and do not resist, they will be carried out by those physically able to do so.
- Uniformed police will not be invited to enter the nave, balconies, or chancel to quell a demonstration during worship. Instead, should the situation become extreme, the congregation will be dismissed and appropriate action taken afterward.

No church record or member's memory indicates that worship was ever ended early because of demonstrators. There is ample evidence, however, that the volunteer, God-loving ushers were "physically able" to deal with disruption.

"I was hit twice in the ass and kicked in the base of the spine," one demonstrator told reporter Sally Quinn of the *Washington Post* after he and an accomplice were dragged from the altar by ushers on October 2, 1977. The two protesters had reached the deepest part of the sanctuary, according to Quinn, and unfurled banners. One read "Can Christians approve nuclear weapons?"

President Carter was at Camp David that morning and missed the invasion. During the coffee hour after worship, Dr. Charles Trentham was shaken, according to the *Post*.

"It is the first incident of this kind we've had," he told Quinn. "Up until now we have tried to keep demonstrators outside of the sanctuary. But in this case I think our ushers had to take charge no matter what their [the protesters'] cause was, whether it was something we were for or against."

Quinn went on: Asked if he planned to take more stringent precautions in the future, Dr. Trentham shook his head in bewilderment. "I don't know," he said. "We're just very vulnerable here. We're really sitting ducks."

Opponents of nuclear weapons were nothing new when Carter

became president and began regularly attending worship services at First Baptist. What was new was widespread awareness of a weapon called the neutron bomb.

On June 6, 1977, the *Washington Post* published an article under an ominous headline: "Neutron Killer Warhead Buried in ERDA Budget." ERDA, the Energy Research and Development Administration, was a short-lived government agency with a mandate to develop solar and wind power and, separately, oversee nuclear weapons research.

The *Post* story became a political nightmare for the Carter Administration. Domestic and international media reaction to the neutron bomb was so intense that the Kennedy School of Government at Harvard University undertook a case study and published a report in 1984 entitled "The Press and the Neutron Bomb."

Less than four months after the *Post*'s first story, "neutron bomb" was in the national vocabulary—and on the protest signs of the first demonstrators to invade First Baptist.

On October 2, 1977, one of the banners lofted at the altar read, "Can we love our enemies with a neutron bomb?" After the worship service, passersby on 16th Street could read a long banner hoisted in front of First Baptist. "Neutron Bomb," it said above a question: "Who will assume moral responsibility?" A photo of the banner filled three columns on page C4 of that Monday's *Washington Post*.

Pastor Trentham was right about the church's vulnerability to protests. Two weeks after the altercation at the altar, more protesters entered the sanctuary, this time blending in among congregants.

"Five persons were arrested yesterday after they staged an anti-neutron bomb protest that temporarily disrupted services being attended by President Carter and his family at the First Baptist Church at 16th and O Streets NW," the *Post* reported on October 17, 1977.

"The five, who identified themselves as members of the Atlantic Life Community, an antiwar group based in Baltimore, rose one at a time from the congregation and attempted to read a statement denouncing the neutron bomb."

Associate Pastor Charles R. Sanks Jr. assured the *Post* reporter that the protesters were assisted in leaving the sanctuary with a "feeling of genuine escort." The reporter had other sources.

"United Press International reported that as the first demonstrator rose to his feet and began to read, a church usher rushed over to him, grabbed the statement and placed his own hand over the demonstrator's mouth," the *Post* account added.

"As the protester was being pulled from a pew, a woman rose in a different section of the church and continued the statement. The scene was repeated each time ushers tried to quell the demonstrators, according to UPI."

Jimmy, Rosalynn and Amy Carter were in the sanctuary for worship during the protests, The *Post* quoted the President as saying that neither he nor the Secret Service felt he was in danger. Carter called the demonstrators "all fine people, and I agree with their purpose to eliminate nuclear weapons," according to the *Post*. "I think they were mistaken in trying to disrupt the church services," he added.

Sanks told the *Post* there was little First Baptist could do to prevent similar outbursts: "No, because we want to keep the church open to all who want to worship. But if we kept it open to all who wanted to speak ... it would be pandemonium."

FROM THE ARCHIVES

The Stationery

At First Baptist D.C., the senior pastor traditionally tends to preaching and lofty spiritual matters, leaving the more administrative tasks of running a church to the associate pastor. President Carter's regular attendance compounded the administrative matters at First Baptist D.C., which is how Associate Pastor Charles R. Sanks Jr. ended up riding herd on reporters, protesters, autograph-seekers and, eventually, his own congregants.

From the minutes of the executive council meeting of First Baptist D.C. on March 12, 1980:

> The Moderator brought up as his last item of business that individuals from our Church had had letters written on Church Stationery to the President of the United States with regard to matters which they thought should be brought to his attention, and the Moderator asked for suggestions as to how best to handle this situation. There was considerable discussion and the consensus of opinion was that Dr. Sanks, as Chief of Staff, should advise the secretaries in the Church Office that any letters prepared which were not from the Church Staff, Chairmen of Committees or Boards, or from the Moderator should be cleared with Dr. Sanks before being done.

Dr. Sanks with President Jimmy Carter on the front steps of First Baptist D.C. *Photo courtesy of the Jimmy Carter Presidential Library*

THE NUCLEAR OPTION

With President and Mrs. Carter present, five men and four women were arrested at First Baptist Church of Washington after they tried to denounce Carter for supporting a first-strike nuclear policy.

WILLIAM F. WILLOUGHBY

WASHINGTON STAR, AUGUST 7, 1978

The selection of the day for the protest, August 6, 1978, was deliberate; the protesters had done their homework. Jimmy Carter's regular attendance at First Baptist D.C. was well known. Less well known was Harry Truman's attendance while he was president.

"At 8:15 a.m. on August 6, 1945, an American B-29 bomber opened its bay doors over the Japanese city of Hiroshima and released a solitary bomb. Forty-four seconds later, it exploded 1,900 feet above the city," the Truman Library Institute wrote in a blog post. "This single explosion brought the Second World War into its final phase and revealed to the world a new and devastating weapon."

On the 33rd anniversary of the first atomic bombing, protesters made their way inside First Baptist and began a coordinated effort to loudly condemn Carter, Truman and the church itself for tolerating the presidents' nuclear inclinations.

Usher Doug Porter was on duty that Sunday, as was church member Robin Clack, then a top official with the Border Patrol. Porter described the chaos in his diary:

President and Mrs. Carter in Class today. Demonstrators invaded Church and made disturbance by trying to read statements in loud voice disrupting the Sunday School Class meeting in the balcony where President Carter is.

Robin Clack had advised them they were welcome to worship with us quietly but that if [there was] any disturbance they would be ejected. One woman immediately arose and commenced to shout. Robin hustled her out and turned her over to police waiting outside.

As soon as Robin had started to take her out, a man who had been sitting next to her rose and started to shout. I came up behind him and locked my arms in his and dragged him out into the aisle. [Another usher] caught the other arm and we took him out the front door and turned him over to the police. Many television cameras were outside. I then returned to my post in the sanctuary.

Toward the end of the regular church service other demonstrators attempted to disrupt the service and were ejected by the ushers. At one point a policeman came in and helped carry out a woman who had gone limp and would not walk out.

The *Washington Star* printed the protesters' statement in the next day's edition:

As persons who seek to follow Christ's teachings, we see the inconsistencies between Christ's words and our American policy of nuclear death-making. ... Can we justify the tremendous expenditure of human energy on making weapons of unthinkable destruction, on a preparation for war, when over half of the human family is suffering from starvation or malnutrition? ... We are called on to worship the God of life, the God of justice, rather than the god of national security.

The *Star* added that "the protesters also denounced the church for remaining silent even though President Harry Truman, who ordered the atomic bomb to be dropped on Hiroshima 33 years ago, was a church member at the time."

Truman attended First Baptist D.C. while president but kept his church membership at his home church in Missouri. As for ordering the bombing of Hiroshima, the Truman Library Institute added an interesting editor's note to its blog:

> No known written record exists in which Harry Truman explicitly ordered the use of atomic weapons against Japan. The closest thing to such a document is a hand-written order, addressed to Secretary of War Henry Stimson, in which Truman authorized the release of a public statement about the use of the bomb. It was written on July 31, 1945, while Truman was attending the Potsdam Conference in Germany. In effect, this served as final authorization for the deployment of the atomic bomb, though the expression "release when ready" refers to the public statement.

———

After the August 1978 incursion, no other reports of disruptions appear in news accounts or First Baptist's archives. Ushers went back to their regular jobs as greeters. Doug Porter was at the front door on April 20, 1980, and described the morning in his diary:

> President and Mrs. Carter came to class today. [The] President greeted me at the church door and Mrs. Carter greeted me with a smile and a cheery "Good Morning."
> The friendly White House man who always carries the satchel, said to contain instructions as to how to proceed in the event of a nuclear threat, greeted me warmly as the Presidential party filed in the front door.

THE 504 DEMONSTRATORS

The handicapped came to Washington hoping they'd get audience with the President or the Secretary of [Health, Education and Welfare]. It doesn't look likely that's about to happen, but they are going to stay and keep trying anyway.

UNIDENTIFIED REPORTER

WE SHALL NOT BE MOVED:

THE 504 SIT-IN FOR DISABILITY CIVIL RIGHTS

AUDIO DOCUMENTARY, JUNE 1997

When Jimmy Carter took office, disabled people in the United States had been waiting more than three years for regulations that would implement Section 504 of the Rehabilitation Act of 1973.

Section 504 plainly prohibits discrimination against "qualified individuals with disabilities" in "any program or activity receiving federal financial assistance."

As with many federal laws, the devil was in the details, specifically the regulations to be written by federal agencies to make the law effective. The job of issuing the first draft of the regulations belonged to the then–Department of Health, Education and Welfare. Amid pushback from employers and other groups affected by the law, Carter's HEW Secretary, Joseph A. Califano Jr., wanted another review of the regulations.

By early 1977, advocates for disabled people were tired of waiting and gave an ultimatum to HEW. When nothing happened, activists —many of them disabled—occupied the HEW offices in a federal building in San Francisco on April 5, 1977, and refused to leave.

As the occupation dragged on, a delegation of San Francisco activists flew to Dulles airport near Washington, D.C., accompanied by Evan White, a San Francisco TV reporter. The people in wheel-chairs traveled from Dulles to the District in the back of a window-less moving van, a scene captured in the 2020 documentary *Crip Camp*.

Their first demonstration was outside Califano's home. On Sunday, April 24, 1977, the demonstrators—some in wheelchairs, some with white mobility canes—came to First Baptist D.C. to see the President. They barely caught a glimpse.

The demonstrators were waiting on 16th Street, across from the church, when the President, Rosalynn and Amy Carter arrived at First Baptist at 9:52 a.m. Reporters—and the demonstrators—took note that the Carter family entered the sanctuary by the side door on O Street and not up the front steps on 16th Street, from where they could easily have seen and heard the demonstrators.

A transcript of the audio documentary, *We Shall Not Be Moved: The 504 Sit-In for Disability Civil Rights*, provided by the Disability Rights Education and Defense Fund, contains details of the day (without the names of reporters on site but with the language of the times):

Unidentified Reporter:

President Carter's church is about four blocks from the church where the handicapped have been staying, close enough for them to make the journey under their own power. When they got there, police and Secret Service let them know they could get no closer than across the street.

They came here with a real, if unrealistic hope, that the President would take the time to come across and perhaps, talk to them. And listen to their plea that pending anti-discrimination regulations be kept strong.

But when he arrived, it was apparent that wasn't about to

happen. And the assumption of the group of two dozen handicapped was that he's using the side entrance of the church for the
first time ever with a very clear message to them: that President
Carter had no intention of getting close.

Judy Heumann, a longtime advocate for disability rights, was
across the street from First Baptist D.C. in her wheelchair. A reporter
recorded her reaction: "I am speechless. I cannot believe that he was
unable to go into the front of the church because 20 of us are sitting
across the street with signs. I wish I knew the politics behind this
situation."

Unidentified Reporter:

Then, the service was completed. The President, this time, used
the church's rear door completely out of sight of the contingent of the
handicapped in front. The presidential car did pass by the group as it
sped away.

Unidentified Reporter:

Rosalynn Carter did wave out the back window. But the President's decision to go out the back door and not acknowledge the
group's presence was naturally met with frustration and disappoint-
ment by those here. As one just mentioned, "We're used to that. The
President didn't want to hear what we had to say; at least he knows
we're here."

Reporter Evan White:

Well, the immediate reaction after the Carter motorcade passed
by ... was that most of the people standing there were crying. It was
one of the toughest situations we've been in, in terms of emotion.

A participant's account from 1977 was reprinted on the website of
the Disability Rights Education and Defense Fund on the 20-year
anniversary of the demonstration:

We never let Carter and Califano forget we were there. We stayed at
Luther Place Church in downtown Washington. No sooner had we
gotten settled in our quarters than we were off for Califano's home

for a candlelight vigil. He went to work that morning via the back door.

This game of hide-and-go-seek went on the entire time. On Sunday we demonstrated across the street from Carter's church. All the while we were watched by security men on the roof of the building next door. Carter avoided facing us by entering the church by a side door and exiting by a rear door. It was at that moment I knew we were going to win the fight. We had spent all week lining up congressional and senatorial support ... and now we had made the President of the United States take it on the lam. That's power.

The presidential daily diary for April 24, 1977, notes that President Carter taught Sunday School after arriving at First Baptist, then attended the worship service. The diary makes no mention of what door he used to leave the church at 12:03 p.m., nor does it mention the demonstrators.

After lunch at the White House that Sunday, President Carter hit the tennis courts, then went with the First Lady to the Kennedy Center for the Performing Arts to dedicate the African Room. After greeting about 450 guests, President and Mrs. Carter went to a potluck dinner at the home of First Baptist's senior pastor. The presidential daily diary made no mention of the demonstrators at any time during the day.

HEW Secretary Califano called President Carter at the White House at 6:14 p.m. Monday, April 25, but didn't reach him; the President was preparing for a dinner with King Hussein of Jordan. Califano got through to the President at 9:12 a.m. Tuesday, April 26; White House logs note a five-minute phone call between the two men. The presidential daily diary for Wednesday, April 27, is blank and marked "Sanitized."

Without reporters or cameras present, Califano signed the regulations implementing Section 504 on April 28, 1977, and the activists ended their occupation of the HEW offices in San Francisco after more than three weeks.

Carter took credit for the regulations in his final State of the Union address on January 16, 1981:

"I hope that my Administration will be remembered ... for

leading the way toward full civil rights for handicapped Americans. When I took office, no federal agency had yet issued 504 regulations. As I leave office, this first step by every major agency and department in the federal government is almost complete."

Carter made no mention of the demonstrators who had so dramatically pushed his administration to take action.

THE SUNDAY SCHOOL CLASS

THE COUPLES CLASS

The day that I first met the President, he said, "I'm looking forward to hearing you teach."

I said, "Well, how about you teaching?" Well, this was only Sunday after the inauguration, and he said, "Well, after all, Fred, I have had a pretty busy week this week," but said, "I will teach."

And he has. And every time that he's taught, he has really blessed our hearts.

FRED GREGG

SUNDAY SCHOOL LESSON

JANUARY 4, 1981

On at least 17 Sundays during his presidency, Jimmy Carter stepped to a lectern in the balcony overlooking the sanctuary of the First Baptist Church of the City of Washington, D.C. There, with his back against one of the concrete pillars that support the soaring neo-Gothic ceiling, Carter faced four rows of long wooden pews beneath the brightly stained glass of the tall Redemption Window.

Shoulder to shoulder in the pews were the adult members of the church's Couples Class, there to hear a Bible lesson from a teacher who just happened to be the President of the United States.

A correspondent for the United Press International reported on February 20, 1977:

> About 70 persons attended the first Sunday School lesson taught by Mr. Carter at the First Baptist Church, which he joined a few weeks ago. A longtime church member said half the class were visitors.
>
> Smiling frequently and talking in low, warm tones, Mr. Carter quoted from the Book of Mark. ... Mr. Carter appeared at ease with the class and held its close attention. He asked members to recite from the Bible and then asked for opinions on what the passages meant.
>
> "How many of you have been on your knees in the past 24 hours?" he asked. "I have."

Carter's four years as president from 1977 to 1981 would be marked by a series of calamitous events that would bring anyone to their knees in prayer, if not despair. Yet, in his Sunday School lessons and other remarks to the Couples Class and—more important—in what he *didn't* say about the cares of his office, President Carter seemed to find a haven at First Baptist D.C., a church home where he could be just another Christian in worship and study.

The class seemed particularly well suited for the President and First Lady. The Couples Class at First Baptist D.C. informally began in late 1943 or early 1944 as young married people moved to Washington for jobs during World War II. The war effort required long, irregular working hours that left little time for couples to be together —except in church. With the blessing of Pastor Edward Hughes Pruden, the Couples Class formally became part of First Baptist's Sunday School on January 5, 1945, with 14 members.

By 1977, the class of working couples was integrated by gender, nationality and race. Among the members were the Liberian ambassador to the United States; the former executive director of the American Public Health Association and his wife, a nurse; an architect; and a patent lawyer. The membership roll for the class contained more than 50 names in alphabetical order except for those of new members, whose names were noted at the top of the list along with their home addresses. For one pair of new members in 1977, the address was 1600 Pennsylvania Ave., Washington, D.C.

On Sunday, January 23, 1977—three days after Carter took the oath of office with his hand on the family Bible—the presidential daily diary included this entry:

> **9:30 a.m.** The President and the First Lady attended a Sunday School couples class. The class was led by Fred M. Gregg, Executive Vice President for Marketing, Equitable Life Insurance Company, Washington, D.C.

FROM THE ARCHIVES

President Carter addresses the Couples Class in the balcony of First Baptist D.C. on November 16, 1980, shortly after he lost his bid for reelection. *Photo courtesy of the Jimmy Carter Presidential Library*

From *First Baptist Church News,* **April 12, 1977**

The President as Teacher

Editor's Note: Caspar Nannes has been retained by the church since February to handle news releases for FBC. Dr. Nannes, before retirement, was Religion Editor of The Washington Star. *The article [below] is an example of his work for our church and was recently released to the Associated Press.*

The telephone rang and Fred M. Gregg, Jr., teacher of the Couples Bible Class at First Baptist Church in Washington, picked up the receiver and identified himself.

"This is Jimmy Carter," the voice at the other end of the line said. "Do you still want me to teach today?"

"Mr. President, you don't know how happy I am to have you teach today. I have had a rough week and have not had much chance to study my lesson."

"I waited until 8 o'clock this morning to call as I have been busy this week and wanted to be sure I could teach today," the Nation's Chief Executive explained.

And with this simple interchange Carter came to teach the Couples Class on Sunday, March 20, two months to the day following his inauguration as President of the United States.

Carter is the first president to teach a bible class while in office, but several of his predecessors taught classes prior to assuming the nation's top position. William McKinley served as superintendent of the Sunday School at First Methodist Church in Canton, Ohio. Theodore Roosevelt taught a class at Christ Episcopal Church in Cambridge, Mass., for three-and-a-half years as a Harvard undergraduate until the Episcopal priest fired him upon learning he was not an Episcopalian but Dutch Reformed and would not change his allegiance.

Carter's introduction to the class was as he would want it, low key. Gregg, a tall and lean grey-haired man with clean-cut features and an attractive southern accent, introduced the President, who had entered unobtrusively and was seated at one end of the spacious balcony overlooking the sanctuary.

Gracefully acknowledging the introduction and after greeting the class, the Man from Plains, Georgia, plunged immediately into teaching the lesson, which revolved around Christ driving the money lenders out of the temple. Totally at ease in his role as teacher, Carter quickly showed that he had carefully prepared the lesson and had planned every step to be studied.

His teaching has a definite technique, born out of years of practice. The President would read a passage, make a few remarks about it, and then encourage the class to ask questions or make comments. This the members did without hesitation, for Carter's informal approach had put them quickly at ease. Alert not to get bogged down on any particular point, he would swiftly move on to another passage once the other section had been adequately discussed.

Carter frequently lightened the serious aspects of the lesson by observations that drew laughter from the class. ...

Finally, bringing the lesson down to the personal, Carter asserted, "No matter how dedicated we might be, the limit of what Christ can be for us individually must come out of our actions, our attitudes, our love. I would like every one of us to feel challenged by a recognition of our own shortcomings and to serve as Christ did."

As we earlier noted, the President obviously enjoys teaching the

Bible. And he broke up his enjoyment by carefully doing his homework and expressing his interpretations with enthusiasm and a willingness to hear what other persons have to say about the passages under discussion. He is a good model for other Bible teachers to emulate.

President Carter at his desk at the White House on a Sunday morning. On his first Sunday at First Baptist, he volunteered to lead Bible study for the Couples Class. Three months later, he wrote in his personal diary that he looked forward to preparing the lessons: "It's time-consuming, but it's something of a religious discipline that I need." *Photo courtesy of the Jimmy Carter Presidential Library*

THE BANQUET

President Jimmy Carter put aside the cares of office the evening of October 14 to join with members of the Couples Class of First Baptist Church of Washington, to which he and Mrs. Carter belong, at the class's 33rd annual banquet.

CASPAR NANNES

FIRST BAPTIST CHURCH NEWS, NOVEMBER 2, 1977

The President's "cares of office" in 1977 started with a natural gas shortage that closed schools and offices during a bitterly cold winter. The long lines at gas stations throughout the United States were fresh in memories. In July, lightning struck power lines and infrastructure serving New York City, cutting power for 25 hours and spawning widespread looting and arson.

In the midst of the crises, the new president tended to the business of his office, including the international hospitality that, for the occupant of the White House, means state dinners: formal affairs involving hundreds of guests, typically honoring the top leader of a foreign government.

The Carters' prowess—and stamina—as hosts earned a toast from *Foreign Policy Magazine*:

"If historians judged presidents purely on their culinary performance, Jimmy Carter would be ranked one of the all-time greats. Not only did he host more state dinners in a single year than any other president—16 in 1977—but on Sept. 7 of that year he also hosted a state dinner with the most guests of honor in history, honoring 27 different Latin American countries in recognition of the United States signing the treaties transferring ownership of the Panama Canal."

Another formal dinner appeared on the Carters' calendar for October 14, 1977. At 7:45 on a rainy Friday night, the First Couple left the White House for First Baptist D.C. and the annual banquet of the Couples Class, held in the basement-level fellowship hall two stories below the sanctuary.

The women wore long dresses; the men, suits and ties. The evening's theme was "Movin' On," and the motif was railroad travel. A hand-drawn train adorned the printed program, and the handmade decorations included cotton balls pinned to the stage curtain to simulate clouds from a locomotive's smokestack.

On the stage, a model train of two engines and four cars circled a collection of small buildings. The label on the train station indicated that the display represented the President's hometown of Plains, Georgia, which prompted Carter's only criticism of the night: "Plains isn't that big," he said.

Informal snapshots of the President at the dinner were taken from a very respectable distance; he's recognizable but tiny in the fading prints. One of the few close-ups might explain the wide berth given the President: a German shepherd dog standing beside the uniformed legs of its handler.

Despite the President's long workday—his first meeting was at 6:45 that morning—the Carters spent a little over 2½ hours with members of the Sunday School class for a few speeches, dinner (but no cocktails or wine—it's a Baptist thing) and singalongs to "Sentimental Journey" and the class song, "Living for Jesus."

In his own remarks, President Carter spoke appreciatively of the class he and Rosalynn had joined barely nine months before the banquet: "You have made our lives normal lives. You have given us stability in a position that is inherently sometimes unstable. A President of our country can be an isolated person. You have taken us in, and we are indebted to you. Thank you very much."

President Carter returned the hospitality about six months later, when he invited members of the Couples Class to the White House for the entertainment portion of a state dinner for Romanian president Nicolae Ceauşescu on April 12, 1978. The Communist leader had helped negotiate the meeting in Israel in November 1977 between President Anwar Sadat of Egypt and Prime Minister Menachem Begin of Israel.

About 10 members of the Couples Class joined presidents Carter and Ceauşescu and other guests in the East Room of the White House for an almost 45-minute performance by British jazz pianist George Shearing.

First Baptist member Doug Porter and his wife, Liz, were at the White House that night. Porter noted the class's appreciation in his diary entry of April 23, 1978: "Thirty Scotch ministers in Class today. President and Mrs. Carter greeted them each personally after Class. Liz told President and Mrs. Carter how much we appreciated being invited to the White House on April 12 to meet the President of Romania. Several couples in the Class were invited at that same time."

FROM THE ARCHIVES

From *Capital Baptist,* **November 10, 1977**

Even a President Needs Love:
President & Mrs. Carter Attend Church Banquet

By Caspar Nannes

President Jimmy Carter put aside the cares of office the evening of October 14 to join with members of the Couples Class of First Baptist Church of Washington, to which he and Mrs. Carter belong, at the class's 33rd annual banquet. ...

The Nation's Chief Executive was introduced to the gathering by Fred M. Gregg, Jr., teacher of the class.

"Mr. President and Mrs. Carter, I want to thank you for the sacrifice you have made to come out to be with us on such a (rainy) night as this," he said.

"You are the ones who sacrificed and we are honored," Carter responded. "We look forward to each opportunity to share your influence and see your welcoming smiles and working with you. It adds a dimension to our lives."

During his remarks, Carter noted that Ambassador Francis Dennis of Liberia, associate teacher of the class, had spoken ahead of him.

Alluding to his friendship with the Ambassador, Carter pointed out that some people have wondered how we could have "the friendship and support of black people of the country. We all had in common a common faith. We all worshiped the same Christ."

He then pointed out a practical result of his relationship with Ambassador Dennis.

"There is a mutual spirit of understanding and care. Kissinger tried three times to get into Nigeria and was refused. Now we have a growing friendship with Nigeria. Whether you are a lonesome boy in Plains, Georgia, or in the White House searching for a new understanding of friendship across the ocean, the thing that binds you together is a belief in Christ."

He then paid tribute to Charles A. Trentham, pastor of First Baptist Church, for his understanding and help.

"We have had some problems with our family as all families do. We have come to Dr. Trentham for advice. This has made us feel not as a President above others, but as a President among others." ...

Carter set the tone for the evening upon his entrance, with a pleasant "Hi everybody" greeting. He then stopped by the tables and shook hands with those near the aisle and later stepped down from the head table with Mrs. Carter to stand by each table while a photographer took their pictures with the class members sitting there. They also posed with those who served the dinner.

Trentham inducted Joseph H. Lyttle for his second term as class president and the other officers in a mass ceremony. Edmund C. Sonnenschein served as toastmaster for the evening.

Douglass M. Porter [the usher and author of the diary] stirred the crowd with his irrepressible singing of favorite songs and Bill Raiford's piano playing, including an original composition, inspired Carter to say, "He has changed completely my image of West Point."

Needless to say, the president is a graduate of the Naval Academy and Raiford of West Point.

Caspar Nannes, on the staff of First Baptist, Washington for feature writing, was formerly religion editor for the Washington Star.

THE TEACHERS

THE SUBSTITUTE

Sometimes I imagine President Carter must go to Sunday school at First Baptist Church of Washington for laughs. He'll get them, a mile a minute, from his Sunday school teacher, Fred Gregg.

WILLIAM F. WILLOUGHBY

WASHINGTON STAR, AUGUST 12, 1978

William F. Willoughby accurately described the sense of humor that Fred Gregg brought to Sunday School at First Baptist D.C., but he overlooked the equally humorous part-time Sunday School teacher who happened to be President of the United States.

Gregg, like Jimmy Carter, was a Southerner, revered in his hometown of Chattanooga as a high school baseball star who made it to the major leagues with Cleveland before going into the insurance industry in Tennessee. At about the same time Carter won the presidency, Gregg landed a new job as executive vice president of the Equitable Life Insurance Company of McLean, Virginia, and moved his family to the suburbs of Washington, D.C.

The new members' list for the Couples Class at First Baptist in early 1977 included Fred and Mary Jo Gregg and Jimmy and Rosalynn Carter.

"I think they connected both personally and spiritually," Hall

Gregg said of her father and Carter. "I really think it came down to their faith. … My father treated him with the respect that a president deserves, but he could kid him without a problem."

The mutual kidding relied heavily on two themes: who was the better Sunday School teacher and the President's pretense that he had to plead for permission to teach. The ribbing was clean and good-natured, but it was, at its heart, trash talk. About Sunday School. And Bible lessons.

Here are excerpts of the comedy stylings of Fred Gregg and the sitting President of the United States, recorded live in the balcony of First Baptist D.C.

March 12, 1978

PRESIDENT JIMMY CARTER:

Well, it's always a pleasure to substitute for the only man I know that has more vacations than Walter Cronkite [the CBS news anchor]. …

I was a little bit hesitant to introduce my own guest. He's my cousin Calvin Carter and his wife, Pat. The thing that makes me reluctant is they're also in the insurance business. They [and Fred] will be trying to sell each other a policy before we get away from the church.

From Doug Porter's Diary, June 18, 1978

President and Mrs. Carter in Class and at Church. Fred Gregg asked the President to give impromptu the highlights of the story of Joseph. He did so and it was given in soft, modest tones, but fully and most interestingly done. When it was through, Fred Gregg jokingly said, "We will now rise and be dismissed," explaining that the President had so perfectly covered all points of the lesson.

December 10, 1978

FRED GREGG:

Now, last Sunday I felt like a hypocrite because I'd prayed all week that the President would call me and would want to teach the

Sunday School class, and he didn't. I wasn't sure exactly how I felt about prayer being answered. But if you'll recall as we got into the lesson that it said that God doesn't always answer our prayers as quickly as we'd like. He wants to make sure we're sincere.

So, I didn't let up. And I kept praying. And last night at 9 o'clock, I got that phone call. The President said, "If you don't mind, I would like to teach tomorrow." I said, "Oh, I couldn't be happier." He said, "If you're prepared, you go right ahead."

And I brought with me my rough notes this morning just to prove to him that I wasn't ready and prepared to teach. I still believe in prayer. But every time that I get this privilege to introduce the President to teach the class, I have greater respect, deeper admiration for this man.

And I still get those cold chills when I say, "President Carter, the class is now yours."

PRESIDENT JIMMY CARTER:

Are you finally ready to let me take it?

I didn't know for a long time what I was going to teach about this morning, but I've been trying for so many weeks to induce Fred Gregg to let me teach that I had really gotten quite aggravated with him. And I didn't know if I'd ever get over it.

I thought this morning I'd take as my subject, "Forgiveness."

March 4, 1979

FRED GREGG:

So I'm not going to take up any more time except to say last Sunday the President asked for a teacher's quarterly and his was locked up, and I had to give him mine, which is kindly tattered and torn.

This morning I said, "Would you like to have yours, or would you like to have one that was tried and tested?"

He handed me mine and said, "I believe I'll give you this one back. It's proved inadequate."

So with that, it gives me a great deal of pleasure to turn the class over to President Carter.

PRESIDENT JIMMY CARTER:

I learned last night that I could be here this morning, and I called Fred and asked him for permission to teach. After thinking it over for a while, he gave me permission.

It's hard to detect delays measured in microseconds, but that's about how long he delayed before he ...

August 5, 1979

PRESIDENT JIMMY CARTER:

I'm going to need a lot of help this morning. Fairly late last night, I had a 15-minute argument with the titular teacher for whom we always substitute, and I finally won the argument, and he agreed to let me teach.

July 20, 1980

PRESIDENT JIMMY CARTER:

Fred just casually left a letter lying here on the podium, I guess wanting me to see it. It's addressed to Reverend Fred Gregg. He'll do anything to let me realize that he is the teacher and I'm the substitute. It's kind of hard to replace a reverend.

November 16, 1980

FRED GREGG:

Mr. President, it's good to have you and Mrs. Carter here this morning. We talked earlier this week, and I told him that he had taught me two things. One, that honesty doesn't always pay. And secondly, that I will be able to explain and describe the resurrection much better, because Tuesday, November the fourth [Election Day], I went numb and didn't resurrect until about the sixth. So there's more than one that has resurrected now.

January 4, 1981
Jimmy Carter's final Sunday with the Couples Class

FRED GREGG:

I know no one knew the President was teaching this morning, and I appreciate so many of y'all coming to hear me. I hate to disappoint you though, but he's going to teach.

THE TROUBLESOME BOOK

It is very difficult for a non-biblical scholar to teach from Revelation because it requires literally a lifetime of studying and prayer and meditation and discussion to understand what Revelation is and what it means to us as Christians.

PRESIDENT JIMMY CARTER
SUNDAY SCHOOL LESSON
MARCH 30, 1980

Revelation, the last book in the Christian Bible, is just plain weird. The fantastical descriptions of creatures and apocalyptic events may have contained meaningful symbols and code words for the earliest Christians suffering from persecution by the Romans, but to current readers, Revelation is like a mash-up of *The Lord of the Rings* and *Deadpool* without a coherent ending.

Nevertheless, the Sunday School curriculum in use at First Baptist D.C. in 1980 put a lesson from Revelation on the calendar for March 30. The members of the Couples Class had to wait a while for the teacher to get to the text.

FRED GREGG:

I came home Friday night to find that the President was coming to Sunday School this morning and also to find that the Sunday School lesson, which I had already discovered last Sunday, was in Revelation. So I immediately began to study and went to bed about 10:30 or 11. Couldn't sleep, got up and decided I'd better wrestle with that a little more.

And yesterday my mother called, and she said, "What are you doing?" And I said, "I'm studying my Sunday School lesson. ... It's in Revelation." She said, "Oh, me." And I didn't know what she meant by that.

And then about two o'clock, [Associate Pastor] Chuck Sanks called, and he said, "Fred, you do know the President's coming?" I said, "Yes." He said, "You do know. Where is the Sunday School lesson?" I said, "It's in Revelation."

He said, "I'll pray for you."

So with that, I went back to studying. At about three o'clock, I just said, "Well, there's something that's got to give here, so I guess the best thing to do is to take a nap." And about a quarter to 5, the telephone rang.

"Did I wake you up?"

I said, "I don't know how you knew it, but you did." [President Carter] said, "Well, the only reason why I knew, I'd just gotten up from my nap."

And he said, "Who's teaching tomorrow?" And I said, "I am." He said, "Well, we need to do better than that."

And he said, "If you're scheduled to teach, I'll take your place." So I know y'all are glad to see me this morning; scoot the podium over here. ...

Now, Mr. President, I promise you, the president of this Sunday School class did not know you were going to teach till five minutes ago, so this crowd is really my crowd. You told me that you may change your mind, so I wanted to be sure.

PRESIDENT JIMMY CARTER:

I have [changed my mind]. I didn't realize you had studied so much.

FRED GREGG:

Let's all stand and be dismissed. …

It is always a pleasure to me, and I know it is to you, for me to turn the Sunday School class over to President Carter.

PRESIDENT JIMMY CARTER:

Hearing that description from Fred about what went on, I hardly recognize it. As a matter of fact, I'm always eager to teach, but Fred is very jealous of his prerogative as the teacher of this class, and it's very hard for me or Ed Sonnenschein or anyone else to have a chance to teach. …

But Fred was nice enough yesterday afternoon to let me teach, and I was honestly not surprised to find when he was so gracious that it was from Revelation.

———

Carter spent much of the next hour struggling to pull a coherent lesson out of the verses from the four chapters of Revelation assigned in the curriculum. The recording of the lesson captures the relief in his voice as he comes to the end. Fred Gregg expressed no sympathy.

PRESIDENT JIMMY CARTER:

Well, I think this is a good lesson as we discern that John is giving a symbolic description, a vision of life for the early Christians and their future life with Christ in heaven. And the same message applies not only in the first century after Christ's death, but also in the 20th century with us.

FRED GREGG:

Well, I know you're glad you came here this morning. Now you visitors, this is one of the substitute teachers. So can you imagine what's in store for you when you come back, when the first team's teaching? Let's all stand and be dismissed.

FROM THE ARCHIVES

In his weekly column on August 12, 1978, Washington Star *religion editor William F. Willoughby offered a general critique of Sunday School —bookended by descriptions of his visit to the Couples Class at First Baptist D.C. He mentions that Sunday School in the United States was more than 150 years old. The first Sunday School class of any flavor in Washington, D.C., was at First Baptist D.C. in 1819. These are excerpts from Willoughby's "Religious News" column, using his original style and punctuation.*

SOMETIMES I IMAGINE President Carter must go to Sunday school at First Baptist Church of Washington for laughs. He'll get them, a mile a minute, from his Sunday school teacher, Fred Gregg.

After a hard week of keeping Menachem Begin and Anwar Sadat at arm's length from one another or keeping some of the people on his staff from hitting the drugs too hard, it must be reassuring for the president to have a place like Fred Gregg's class to go to.

Once in awhile the president teaches the class, and last Sunday I went to the class on the notion that he might possibly be the teacher. Well, as it turned out he and Rosalynn were students—if that is what one honestly can call someone who attends a Sunday school class. There were about 100 persons there, most of them over the hill like me.

I certainly didn't go because I like Sunday school as a way to spend one's time. I prefer, instead, to read a good book on theology or something akin to it in the time ordinarily allotted for Sunday school. …

AS LONG AS I CAN remember I have never liked Sunday school, and I can't say that being in the same class with the president and the first lady changes the characteristics of a Sunday school class enough for me to want to go back on anywhere near a regular basis. I enjoyed the fact that they were there, however. I certainly am a backer of the president's brand of religion and occasionally I even find I agree with some of his political gambits.

It's not that Fred Gregg's class isn't a winner. He's a downright entertaining and if you take what he has to say to heart, a profitable teacher. In fact, there were quite a few good things said.

But how do you like something you don't like? I know that as an evangelical I am supposed to love Sunday school just as much as I love God, Mother and country. ...

I WISH IT WERE different. There must be at least a million Sunday school classes that are taught every Sunday in this country, and I'll guarantee that the vast majority of them would never make it as educational media. And that's after more than 150 years since the Sunday school movement took hold in this country.

That's bad, because it means the best single opportunity to teach a youth or most adults something really substantial from the Bible is shot. Forty-five minutes at a time....

Gregg's Sunday school class has quite a good offering, well couched in fundamentalist-types of expressions that make it real nice and down-homey. Much of what he says is very stimulating. And humorous. I played back my tape recording of the class and found myself laughing up a storm right along with the president and first lady and the rest of the one hundred.

FRED SAID TOO MANY of us get "all tied up with keeping up with the Joneses" to the point that we forget about putting our full effort into being witnesses for our faith. That's a bad state of affairs, Fred said.

"Just about the time you git caught up, they've done gone and refinanced agin." And with Fred's intensely Southern drawl, the way he says it is almost as entertaining as what he says.

The president's Sunday school teacher has a good way of firing up people and I heard him on a particularly good day. I heard the president go up to him and tell him, "You were in your stride today. You were at your very best." His lesson was on the need for Christian witnessing.

Fred comes by his teaching quite naturally. He's executive vice president for marketing for the Equitable Life Insurance Company in McLean. His job is to get about 800 men fired up to the point they can sell insurance to anyone and everyone. Well, he's trying to sell another kind oi insurance on Sundays, a policy I wish every person in the world held—despite how fundamentalist that sounds.

THE MISSIONARY

I haven't had a chance to consult with Fred [Gregg] this morning to see if I'm going to be able to finish out my term as president or not before I go to Africa full-time as a Christian missionary.

SUNDAY SCHOOL LESSON
JANUARY 29, 1978

President Jimmy Carter came to church on January 29, 1978, packing a double barrel of steely sarcasm. That morning's *Washington Star* carried an interview with Sunday School leader Fred Gregg, in which Gregg opined that Carter would become a missionary to Africa after his presidency. Carter unloaded as soon as Gregg relinquished the lectern. "I sure noticed a difference in the tone of that introduction from the ones that I generally get—aspersions about having a secondary or an inferior substitute this morning and so forth.

"And the reason is that Fred's very proud of the fact that he has announced to the press what I was going to do with the rest of my life."

The class broke out in laughter, but Carter wasn't done with his deadpan takedown.

"I haven't had a chance to consult with Fred this morning to see if I'm going to be able to finish out my term as president or not before I go to Africa full-time as a Christian missionary. But that's what happens when you get a teacher that has a lot of competition from his substitute. He immediately just starts trying to think of ways to get rid of you. But I'm not leaving."

Despite Carter's tongue-in-cheek rebuke of his friend that Sunday, the President was deeply interested in missionary work, also known as spreading the gospel. Carter, like many Christians, believed that Jesus Christ was such a personally transforming presence in his life that he was compelled and commanded to share the good news.

An active Southern Baptist at the time, Carter was well aware of the denomination's organized networks of domestic and foreign missionaries, but he was also familiar with—and a little envious of— the missionary work of the Mormons and Presbyterians,

(Some readers may wonder why Christians sharing the same story about Jesus Christ would care which denomination was better at doing it. If I find the answer, I'll write another book.)

Early in his presidency, Carter spent time exploring the model of the Mormons, officially the Church of Jesus Christ of Latter-day Saints. On March 20, 1977, Carter wrote in his personal diary, "I taught Sunday school and broached the idea to the Sunday school class, from which no action is to be expected, that Baptists and other evangelical groups ought to adopt the same policy that the Mormon Church has: to send large numbers of young men and women volunteers around the world for a year or two of service to the church, working with missionaries. I have an inclination to pursue this more in the future, when I have time to put my thoughts together."

Less than a month later, on April 17, 1977, Carter followed up on his idea, phoning the president of the church in Salt Lake City, Utah, then meeting with Fred Gregg. Carter summed up his interest in his diary:

"The total Protestant denominations' missionary effort consists of about 25,000 people. The Mormon Church alone, their volunteer short-term effort, recruits about 26,000. I'd like to see the Baptist Church take this on as a major undertaking if we can work it out, and Fred Gregg's going to Nashville to talk to the Southern Baptist Convention leaders this week."

Gregg returned from Nashville to report a positive reception to the President's idea, and Carter doubled down on his missionary plan. On June 7, 1977, between meetings on funding the B-1 bomber and the effect of his energy policies on Alaska, the President hosted an hour-long luncheon meeting at the White House with Baptist leaders to discuss his vision.

"[H]e stressed that what he is proposing is something new and different and over and above the regular denominational program," the DC Baptist Convention reported in its newsletter, *Capital Baptist*. Carter "envisioned literally thousands of Baptists, ranging from young people to persons in retirement, who would devote two years exclusively to this specific work of the Lord."

The *Capital Baptist* reported that no details emerged from the meeting, but by a week later, on June 14, 1977, a full plan for a new horde of Baptist missionaries was on paper and ready for a vote by the 16,271 messengers, or delegates, to the annual meeting of the Southern Baptist Convention in Kansas City, Missouri.

The convention's executive committee recommended a plan to enlist and support 5,000 mission volunteers by 1982. Fred Gregg introduced the recommendation with help from a videotaped message from President Carter. The recommendation was approved, but the corps of mission-minded Baptists never materialized.

"This proposal for volunteer missionaries was supported by [Southern Baptist] President Jimmy Allen and adopted by the Southern Baptist Convention, but the commitment was largely abandoned after more fundamentalist leaders gained control in 1979," Carter wrote in an addendum to his personal diary.

Carter's failure to mobilize an army of missionaries didn't detract from his own efforts to spread the gospel. On a state visit to South Korea in late June and early July 1979, Carter mixed official business with church business, welcoming Christian leaders to the U.S. embassy and marveling, later, at the most successful missionary denomination in South Korea.

"Does anybody know what denomination?" Carter asked his Sunday School class in August 1979. "You may not believe it. Presbyterians. They got started earlier, and they are the envy, in a nice way, of the Catholics and the Baptists and the Methodists and everybody else."

Carter went on to relate his attendance at a revival service led by Billy Graham and his meeting with a Korean evangelist, Billy Kim.

"[Kim] said, 'Would you do me a favor?' Carter recounted. "He says, 'When you meet with President Park [Chung Hee] would you witness to him about our Christian faith?' And I said, 'Okay.'

"So as we rode from the Blue House, which is the same as our White House, back to the airport, nobody was in the car except me and President Park and an interpreter and the security guard. And I told him about our faith, and he was very interested.

"And I said, 'I'm sorry we don't have more time together. Would you let one of our Christian friends come and talk to you about it more?' And he said, 'Yes.'...

"So I wrote Billy Kim a little note and ... wrote President Park a little note. And I don't know what will come of it, but so be it. It's in God's hands. But this is a kind of little incident that can happen between two presidents, but that's no more important in the eyes of God than you and your next-door neighbor."

Carter concluded the state visit with an invitation for the South Korean president to come to Washington, but Park was assassinated less than four months later.

———

Despite his missionary inclinations, Carter was having none of the suggestions made by Fred Gregg in his interview published in the *Washington Star* in January 1978. The President had an idea of his own: "I'm having a press conference tomorrow morning, and I'm going to announce what Fred's going to do with the rest of his life ... including the immediate disposition of his financial estate. ... If you all have any suggestions for me before tomorrow morning, let me know."

When the class stopped laughing, Carter got serious—if not a little melancholy—before taking a couple of gentle pokes at Gregg and himself. "Fred and I have had a great and growing personal friendship, as all of you know, and we see the personal involvement of all of us and a greatly expanded Christian mission program as being an integral part of a Christian's life.

"Fred, I thank you for your friendship and what you mean to me. It's good to have a Sunday School teacher that becomes an instant part of your personal and family life, particularly when you are living in the White House, and you've severed a lot of your relationships back home that provided stability for you. Our pastor and our Sunday School teacher have performed that function in the life of my family.

"[Fred] always seems to pick out the difficult subjects for me to teach. This [Sunday] was Jesus and the Holy Spirit. Jesus and the Spirit. And there are a lot of people here present this morning that could do a much better job of teaching this lesson than I can, but I'm going to call on them for help."

With that, President Carter plunged into teaching a Bible lesson from John 14:15, asking a class member to read Jesus' clear direction to his followers from the Revised Standard Version of the New Testament: "If you love me, you will keep my commandments."

FROM THE ARCHIVES

THE TROUBLESOME INTERVIEW

From the Washington Star, *January 19, 1978*

Missionary Career Ahead for Carter?

By Lawrence McQuillan
United Press International

When President Carter leaves the White House, he plans to become a foreign missionary for the Southern Baptists in hopes he might turn a country "back to God and ... our side," his Sunday Bible school teacher says.

Fred Gregg, who teaches the adult bible class attended by the president and first lady Rosalynn Carter at the First Baptist Church of Washington at 16th and O Streets NW, said Carter told him of his plans during a discussion of missionary efforts.

Gregg, an insurance executive, quoted Carter as telling him recently that "when I get out of the White House, I plan to go for a year or two" as a missionary.

"I want you to go for a year or two when you retire ... we're trained, we've taught Sunday school," Carter told Gregg.

The President, who teaches the class once every four to six weeks, has made a public plea for more Southern Baptist missionaries.

"Now if we go to some country where there is a language barrier, I'd like for us to give three or four months training just in how to communicate," Gregg quoted the president as saying.

"He said, 'My mother did that when she went over to India, and she was in her 60s,' " Gregg said in an interview. The president's mother, Miss Lillian, worked in India as a Peace Corps volunteer.

Gregg quoted Carter as saying, "I don't want to wake up 10 or 15 years from today and find a country that is friendly to us, that has turned to the other side, just because some missionary did not do the job he could have done.

"He said, 'I would like to be a part of being able to turn that country back to God and back to our side and I hope someday that that's what I'll get to do,' " Gregg recalled.

Gregg, who said he and the president have prayed together in the private family quarters of the White House, presented a personal plea for missionaries from Carter last year during a gathering of the Southern Baptist Convention in Kansas City.

Carter has said Southern Baptists should put heavier emphasis on missionaries who work for a limited period of time, rather than limiting their major thrust to those who make it a lifetime calling.

THE LESSONS IN THE BALCONY

THE READER

I don't know what I'm going to do as a teacher when I have to look at those seats and know that they're not there, and when I need someone to read, I'm going to have to wait till somebody finds it, and I won't have Rosalynn to flip to it right quick and read it without me losing my concentration.

FRED GREGG

LEAD SUNDAY SCHOOL TEACHER

JANUARY 4, 1981 (THE CARTERS' FINAL SUNDAY AT FIRST BAPTIST D.C.)

Rosalynn Carter was a regular in Sunday School and worship at First Baptist D.C., just not as regular as her husband. She was busy.

One month after the inauguration, on February 20, 1977, President Carter attended Sunday School and church with the First Lady and later lamented in his diary: "Rosalynn is overworked, has too small a staff, and is called on to do an enormous amount of entertaining for official visits. She's also formed the Commission on Mental Health, is taking Spanish lessons three hours a day, the speed-reading course, and has an almost unbelievable amount of press coverage and requirements for her appearances at special events. A lot of that work would be on my shoulders if she were not willing and confident to take it."

The archives of First Baptist D.C. provide only glimpses of the

First Lady at First Baptist, from a few mentions in Doug Porter's diary to photos in the *First Baptist Church News,* where she's pictured smiling as the church youth choir performs Christmas concerts at the White House, to snapshots of her mingling with guests at the annual banquet of the Couples Class.

As mother to nine-year-old Amy, Mrs. Carter was waiting on the steps to the baptismal pool with dry clothes and a hair dryer after her daughter's baptism on February 6, 1977, according to news accounts. She was also present for another rite of childhood about 17 months later, Doug Porter noted in his diary: "Irene Fatula sat behind the Carters in Church and said that Amy tugged at her tooth during the service. When she pulled it out, she crawled over two or three people and handed it to the President. He looked at it a few moments and then handed it to Mrs. Carter who examined it and then put it in her purse."

Rosalynn Carter's own mother, Allie Smith of Georgia, joined her at First Baptist several times, according to Porter and the presidential daily diary. Just as frequently, the First Lady was away on official business. Porter noted some of those events in his diary:

> **December 18, 1977:** President Carter taught lesson in Class today [from] John 11. Mrs. Carter left early for interview with Barbara Walters.

> **August 13, 1978:** Present Carter shook my hand as he came into Class today and gave it a good squeeze and flashed a good smile. … After class President mingled with class members and visitors more freely than usual and made a point of greeting as many as he could. Rosalynn Carter was not present since she is in Rome attending the funeral of Pope Paul VI.

> **March 25, 1979:** Mrs. Carter and her mother, Mrs. Smith, were in Class and Church today, also Amy and the Carter Baby.

Shirley McBeath and her husband, Dr. William McBeath, were members of the Couples Class as well as friends of the Carters. Mrs. McBeath recalled a Sunday when Rosalynn Carter "came in the front door with a baby, and handed him to me to take to the nursery. Can you imagine? Just handing off the President's grandson!"

Dr. McBeath was executive director of the American Public Health Association, founded in 1872 to advocate for public health policies and promote public awareness of community health. In 1978, the association awarded one of its top honors, the Presidential Citation, to Rosalynn Carter for her work promoting mental health as First Lady and serving as honorary chair of the Presidential Commission on Mental Health.

There was only one problem with the award: The First Lady was too busy to get to the association's annual meeting to receive it. So her Sunday School classmates, Bill and Shirley McBeath, took it to her at the White House.

Rosalynn Carter (center) speaks with fellow church members on the steps of First Baptist D.C. At the First Lady's left is her friend Shirley McBeath. *Photo courtesy of the Jimmy Carter Presidential Library*

On January 4, 1981, the Carters' final Sunday with the Couples Class, the President asked the First Lady to read the Scripture for the day's lesson. The Scripture was Luke 9:37-62, and the lesson was titled "Following Jesus' Example."

"President and Mrs. Carter were much beloved, and First Baptist Church members felt so honored to have them as active members," Mrs. McBeath said in an interview. "They gave us energy and hope and changed our lives forever. They have since lived to show the world what solid and serving, loving and caring people they are. As we at First Baptist Church would say, they are truly Christ-like."

FROM THE ARCHIVES

THE DISASTERS

The Carter family—Jimmy, Rosalynn and Amy, along with Amy's nanny —arrived at First Baptist D.C. shortly before 10 a.m. on November 6, 1977. Within a few minutes, they learned of a catastrophe in their home state: A dam had collapsed above Toccoa Falls Bible College in far northeastern Georgia.

"About 1:30 a.m. Sunday, after days of torrential rains, the dam started to leak," the college recounts on its website. "Groaning under the pressure of 129 million gallons of water, the leak became a breach, and the dam washed away, sending a 30-foot wall of water roaring through the trailer park and Bible college in the peaceful valley below.

"In a few horrifying minutes, at least 39 men, women, and children died in the onslaught of rushing water, wreckage and mud."

Less than three weeks earlier, Rosalynn and Jimmy Carter had agreed that she would be his representative at disasters. After Sunday School, worship and lunch on November 6, Mrs. Carter boarded a jet for Georgia.

While President Carter spoke by telephone with the governor of Georgia, the First Lady toured the flood area by helicopter and met with reporters, including a correspondent for the *Washington Post*. " 'Jimmy wanted me to come here to express his concern,' she said. 'The federal government will cooperate in any way possible under the law,' to provide aid. 'It is a terrible tragedy. You have my support and Jimmy's support as you rebuild.' "

The *New York Times* covered the flood and the First Lady's visit on its front page the following day, then published a follow-up story on Tuesday by correspondent B. Drummond Ayres, who got close to the scene of the disaster:

Whether in Johnstown. Pa., or Rapid City, S.D., flood debris normally looks the same—crumpled cars, splintered trees, smashed furnishings and mud, mud, mud. But the debris of the Toccoa Creek disaster is different.

This time there are Bibles—black and red and leather, new and worn and ripped, open to Genesis, Second Samuel,

Matthew. They are caught in bushes, buried in children's toys and still on shelves, with the gold lettering of their bindings smudged by the waters.

———

A little more than seven months after the Toccoa flood, President Carter notified Congress of his plans to consolidate the federal government's roles in disaster response and preparedness.

"The present situation has severely hampered Federal support of State and local emergency organizations and resources, which bear the primary responsibility for preserving life and property in times of calamity," Carter wrote on June 19, 1978. "This reorganization has been developed in close cooperation with State and local governments."

On March 31, 1979, Carter signed Executive Order 12127, effective April 1,1979, establishing the Federal Emergency Management Agency. Over the final 21 months of Carter's presidency, FEMA responded to 62 major disasters, including hurricanes, tornadoes, flooding and the eruption of Mount St. Helens in May 1980.

Mount St. Helens erupted on May 18, 1980, in the deadliest volcanic explosion in U.S. history. *Photo courtesy of USGS Photographic Library*

THE CHRISTIAN, THE MUSLIM
AND THE JEW

President Carter was to teach Class today but let Fred Gregg know that he would still be involved in the Camp David meeting.

DOUG PORTER DIARY ENTRY

SEPTEMBER 17, 1978

One week after Jimmy Carter missed his turn as Sunday School teacher, he was back before the Couples Class. The Associated Press reported that "the president, in his new role as peacemaker, won a standing ovation from his Bible class at the First Baptist Church before he taught the weekly lesson."

The lesson for September 24, 1978, was "Facing Tensions," based on Philippians 4. Before turning to the text, President Carter opened with a personal story of tensions during the 13 days he spent at Camp David with Egyptian President Anwar Sadat and Israeli Prime Minister Menachem Begin:

> I think some of the most unpleasant moments of my life occurred during the last two weeks and, of course, also some of the most pleasant.
>
> One of the great things about the meeting was that I was meeting with two leaders who were deeply devout and religious men. Who

spent a great portion of their time at Camp David in prayer. Who believe that they and I worship the same God.

President Sadat refers often to his guidance from God Almighty. The fact that he and Begin are both descended from Abraham, that they're brothers, not only in religious beliefs, but also by blood.

And that was one of the things that I believe gave us a kind of a clear, unshakable purpose, because we all believed that God wanted us to work toward peace. It was one of the few things on which we agreed at first.

Carter and his staff made sure all three men had time and space to worship and pray at Camp David. Back in Washington, 68 miles south of Camp David, a whole lot of praying took place at First Baptist before, during and after the peace summit.

News cameras and reporters surrounded Carter on Sunday, November 20, 1977, as he left an early morning prayer service at First Baptist. He skipped the worship service to get back to the White House and watch the live broadcast of Sadat addressing the Israeli Knesset, or parliament.

Carter was back for another special prayer service at First Baptist on September 3, 1978.

"At that noontime service, special prayers for World Leaders, for World Hopes, for World Well-being, and for World Cultures were offered by a Jewish Rabbi, a Moslem [sic] religious leader, and two Baptist Ministers," the *Capital Baptist* reported in an outbreak of odd capitalization.

An unknown writer for the *First Baptist Church News* was more circumspect and descriptive:

A service of prayers was held at First Baptist Church immediately following worship and communion on Sunday, September 3.

The event was made possible when Rabbi Joshua O. Haberman, a leading rabbi and renowned leader of the Washington Hebrew Congregation, and Dr. Muhammad Abdul-Rauf, Director of Washington's Islamic Center, accepted our invitations to pray together with us in a special service for peace in the Middle East. When we informed President Carter of the upcoming service, he expressed his deep appreciation and said that he would be present.

Many who attended expressed wonder and joy for having participated in a service where the prayers of three world-wide faiths were offered to Almighty God in unity of purpose for human well-being. Such singleness of intent was strikingly evident in the prayers of Dr. Trentham, Rabbi Haberman, Dr. Abdul-Rauf and Dr. Sanks.

President Carter was so moved by the event that at the conclusion he went into the chancel to express personally his appreciation to the leaders of the service.

There is sincere gratitude within our congregation for the role that is ours in world events. Soon there will be an announcement of additional opportunities for our fellowship and our community to participate in meaningful ways toward peace in the world.

Twenty-four hours after the service at First Baptist ended, Carter boarded Marine One for a 32-minute helicopter flight to Camp David and 13 days of negotiation that culminated in the peace agreement between Egypt and Israel, still in effect today.

For their work, Anwar Sadat and Menachem Begin were awarded the Nobel Peace Prize in December 1978. Jimmy Carter received the prize in December 2002.

FROM THE ARCHIVES

On Sunday, September 10, 1978, negotiations were at an impasse. After a brief worship service, President Carter joined the Israeli and Egyptian leaders in a motorcade to Gettysburg, Pennsylvania, where they spent two hours touring the Civil War battlefield. The stops included the Virginia monument, where a park ranger spoke to Egyptian President Anwar Sadat (on Carter's right) and Israeli Prime Minister Menachem Begin (on Carter's left), their aides, Rosalynn Carter and Mrs. Begin.

Photo courtesy of the Jimmy Carter Presidential Library

THE BAPTIST FROM KYIV

[Georgi] Vins is neither a political dissident, nor a human rights advocate, nor a Jew seeking emigration—the three types of gulag prisoners we hear most about. He is the pastor of a small Baptist church who twice refused the Soviets' offer of voluntary deportation. Instead, he was imprisoned for his work in the illegal Reform Baptist Church and spent eight of the last thirteen years sleeping on concrete floors and subsisting on barley extract, tea and soup.

JOHN BLOOM

TEXAS MONTHLY, AUGUST 1979

Forty-five years before the Biden administration negotiated a complicated, multinational prisoner exchange for the freedom of *Wall Street Journal* reporter Evan Gershkovich and others, the administration of President Jimmy Carter swapped two convicted spies for five Soviet detainees.

Among those freed from Soviet internment in April 1979 were journalist Alexander Ginzburg and Georgi Vins, a Baptist pastor from Kyiv whose "crime" was refusing to affiliate with a government-endorsed organization of Baptist churches. Vins believed staunchly in the separation of church and state—a passion he shared with President Carter.

"The dramatic and unexpected exchange took place at about 3:30 p.m. in hangar 17 of Kennedy International Airport in New York, where the five landed from Moscow on a regularly scheduled flight of Aeroflot, the Soviet national airline," reporter Edward Walsh wrote in the *Washington Post*.

Later in his account, Walsh noted that "White House press secretary Jody Powell announced the exchange, the result of about six months of negotiations, with obvious satisfaction but a minimum of official fanfare." Powell's announcement, read to reporters in the White House briefing room at 3:50 p.m. April 27, 1979, was three sentences long.

Other White House documents flesh out the President's reaction to the news. The official presidential daily diary noted that at about the time the Aeroflot plane landed, President Carter started a seven-minute conference call with Jimmy R. Allen, then president of the Southern Baptist Convention, and Dr. Charles Trentham, Carter's pastor at First Baptist D.C. Trentham had met with Pastor Vins' wife in Kyiv during a trip to the Soviet Union in the summer of 1978.

After that call, "Allen sent a telegram to SBC state executives and presidents, stating, 'President Carter called to rejoice with us that through his tough negotiations for months, our brother in Christ, pastor Georgi Vins, and his family have been released from the Soviet Union. The prayers of our people have been answered," according to Baptist Press accounts summarized in the *Capital Baptist* newsletter.

Less than 48 hours after the Aeroflot flight landed in New York, Pastor Vins, his interpreter and Jimmy Allen were in the balcony of First Baptist D.C. with the church's Couples Class.

On April 29, 1979, President Carter taught a lesson titled "A Cry for Justice" with a Scripture passage from 1 Kings, both prescribed by the preset Sunday School curriculum but whose relevance for that Sunday was unmistakable. Even Carter was surprised.

"Up early to prepare my Sunday school lesson, from 1 Kings 21—about Ahab, Jezebel, and Naboth. Since Georgi Vins was with me, the parallel between this lesson and his persecution in the Soviet Union was remarkable," Carter wrote in *White House Diary*.

Marjorie Hyer, the religion editor of the *Washington Post*, covered Carter's lesson:

Soviet dissident Georgi P. Vins, newly arrived in the United States, attended President Carter's Sunday school class yesterday and found himself likened to the just man in the day's Old Testament lesson who was persecuted for his faithfulness to God's teachings.

Inevitably, as the president developed the lesson, the Soviet Union was cast in the role of the ruthless biblical ruler of ancient Israel who permitted oppression and deceit to gain his ends.

At no time did the president, who volunteers to teach the Couples' Class at First Baptist Church every few weeks, mention the Soviet Union by name, but his repeated allusions to Vins' willingness to suffer for his convictions made the analogy obvious.

Actually, Carter mentioned the Soviet Union twice, but only in the introduction to his guest and the Bible lesson. Carter said:

I've just been told that four days ago, Pastor Vins was in a cattle car being transported within Siberia as an exile in his own country because of his belief in Christ and because of his own personal courage in expressing that belief in the strongest and most forceful way, in spite of the intense pressure and punishment placed on him and his family by the Soviet officials.

There could hardly be a better lesson than what I've already said. Coincidentally, perhaps, or because of the works of God in some strange and mysterious way, our lesson today is precisely a lesson about our visitor: his life in the Soviet Union, his altercation with state officials, his intense courage, his punishment. And I guess it is a coincidence, but I'm not quite sure.

April the 29th, 1979, and in our Sunday School text, the title of our subject is "A Cry for Justice." And the lesson comes from 1 Kings, the 21st chapter. And if you would open your Bibles there, we will follow along for a while discussing Ahab, Jezebel, Naboth, and the prophet Elijah. And then later we will talk about the lesson that we can derive from this text as we discuss these personal verses.

As he did frequently, President Carter then directed the class's attention to the practical application of the day's text. "And I would particularly want you this morning not to think about the time of Ahab, not to think about even the Soviet Union, but to think about the United States, the Washington, D.C., community, and preferably, my life and your life, and our actions in the eyes of God."

Forty minutes later, President Carter brought the lesson to a close and prepared to meet one-on-one with Georgi Vins in the pastor's study at First Baptist. Before he left the class, Carter delivered another nudge toward practicality. "Ahab was sinful. Jezebel was sinful. The people who stayed silent were sinful in the face of injustice—Naboth's neighbors; the Jewish council of elders, who held a trial; those who threw the first stones, which had to be those who testified against him.

"It's sinful to be silent in the face of injustice," President Carter concluded. "And I would like to remind you and be reminded myself that the people of God who know Christ must represent the cause of justice on behalf of the oppressed everywhere."

President Carter meets with Ukrainian pastor Georgi Vins and an unidentified interpreter in the pastor's study at First Baptist D.C. after Vins attended a Bible lesson taught by Carter. Less than 48 hours earlier, Vins had arrived in the United States after being released from Soviet custody. *Photo courtesy of the Jimmy Carter Presidential Library*

THE VOTE

I was hoping that when Fred [Gregg] was saying what a great president history would judge me to be that he would say something about my teaching ability, but I notice he didn't mention that.

PRESIDENT JIMMY CARTER

SUNDAY SCHOOL LESSON

NOVEMBER 16, 1980

On November 12, 1980, members of First Baptist D.C. gathered for their quarterly business meeting. On the agenda for a vote was a message for two specific members. It was approved unanimously and delivered the following Sunday by the church's top lay leader, Moderator Frank Ed McAnear.

In a separate vote less than two weeks earlier, Jimmy Carter was trounced in his bid for re-election, losing by a landslide to Ronald Reagan. Carter was in the balcony at First Baptist on November 16, when McAnear stepped to the lectern.

"Last Wednesday evening at our quarterly business meeting, the membership of our church passed unanimously a resolution," the moderator said. "That message is entitled 'A Message of Love and Support for President and Mrs. Carter.' And I'd like to read it for you at this time."

McAnear went on to read a five-paragraph message with two unmistakable points: The members of First Baptist D.C. were 100 percent supportive of Jimmy Carter as a Christian and far less than 100 percent supportive of Jimmy Carter as president. But the message was very nicely worded.

Carter accepted a copy with aplomb: "I'm not going to get emotional because we'll be here two more months, and I can't sustain it that long," he said, then paused. "It is always remarkable when Baptists pass something unanimously." The class broke into laughter. "That makes a beautiful message and the proclamation even more dear to us because it's so rare."

Carter then went on to teach his penultimate Sunday School class, drawn primarily from Luke 5 and entitled "Grace for Sinners."

As for the congregation's message, Carter wrote a formal thank-you note to the members of First Baptist on November 25, 1980—two days before Thanksgiving. A facsimile, complete with the President's distinctive signature, filled the first page of the church newsletter on Christmas Eve 1980:

Rosalynn joins me in thanking you for your thoughtful message. We treasure the fellowship and friendship we have enjoyed with you over the past four years.

Your prayerful support and "the ties that bind our hearts in Christian love" will be remembered, along with your many kind-nesses, long after we have returned to our home in Georgia.

With our warm regards to each of you.

Sincerely,
Jimmy Carter

FROM THE ARCHIVES

A Message of Love and Support
for President and Mrs. Jimmy Carter

Almost four years ago you became with us, fellow members of the Body of Christ in this place. Although none of us could begin to realize the awesome burden of your public office, we all joined in a continuing fellowship of prayer for you and for our nation's first family, for you and for members of our congregation. This love and care continues even until now.

We have wanted to share with you the resources of faith and devotion to a cause which transcends all political parties—the kingdom of our Lord, and of his Christ. Being good Baptists we have been aware that our freedom to differ politically has not destroyed the more fundamental Christian commitment that we all share. To our diverse congregation you have brought an appreciation for the presence of fellow Christians who give themselves to political leadership in the nation.

Now, none of us can imagine the feelings in your hearts after the election, but still all of us—devoted citizens of many political persuasions—understand the meaning of the commandment of the apostle to "bear one another's burdens and so fulfill the law of Christ."

Therefore, we wish to say simply and directly that our love and prayerful support are with you. Even those who may have differed from you in matters political shall treasure the association with you in these years together and pledge continually to work with you in the spread of the gospel of our Lord.

We pray for you—and for ourselves—that we may attain the peace which passes understanding and the joy which can lighten every day in Christ our Lord.

Your friends and partners in the gospel,
The First Baptist Church of the City of Washington, DC.

First Baptist Church News

| Washington, D.C. | December 24, 1980 | Vol. 32, No. 22 |

THE WHITE HOUSE

WASHINGTON

November 25, 1980

To the Members of the First Baptist Church
of the City of Washington, D.C.

Rosalynn joins me in thanking you for your
thoughtful message. We treasure the fellowship
and friendship we have enjoyed with you over
the past four years.

Your prayerful support and "the ties that bind
our hearts in Christian love" will be remembered,
along with your many kindnesses, long after we
have returned to our home in Georgia.

With our warm regards to each of you,

Sincerely,

Jimmy Carter

NEW YEAR'S EVE AT FIRST BAPTIST

Dinner at 8:30 p.m., $5.00 for adults; $2.00 for dependent children
Talent Show following dinner in Fellowship Hall
Communion Service, 11:30 p.m., in the Sanctuary
(Reservations for dinner must be made by Monday, December 29.)

THE FINAL LESSON

President and Mrs. Carter came early to Sunday School today because our class had a little reception in the parlor to bid them farewell and to show our appreciation for having had them in our class for these four years. They just couldn't have been nicer. They mingled around amid all the folks, chatting and smiling and greeting everybody. I thanked him for the inspiration he has given and for the example he has been through it all. We all returned to class where he taught the lesson. And it was the last.

Doug Porter Diary Entry

January 4, 1981

On the frigid first Sunday of 1981, the Couples Class at First Baptist D.C. opened with remarks by various members, a prayer by a former class teacher and the customary comments of regular teacher Fred Gregg, who spent several minutes describing a recent fall from a ladder onto his driveway. Gregg was uninjured but sore and, of course, joking throughout.

Carter was in worse shape: He had broken his left collarbone a week earlier while cross-country skiing at Camp David and was wearing a harness prescribed by the White House physician that immobilized his left arm. His humor was undamaged. "I told Fred

I'll wrestle with him to see who taught today," Carter said. "He didn't even think it was funny."

The President spent 2½ minutes describing his impending departure from Washington and his return to Plains, Georgia. He expressed appreciation to the Couples Class and then, characteristically, got down to business. "We have a responsibility this morning to, I think, forget about goings and comings of class members and revert back to the teaching of the Bible," Carter said. "And if all of you would turn to Luke 9, I'll let you help me with the lesson."

About 40 minutes later, Carter closed his final Sunday School class at First Baptist D.C. The last words of his lesson are inscribed on a brass plaque affixed to the pillar that protected his back in the church balcony: "If we'll just act like Jesus, we'll be good Christians. And if we try hard, God will understand when we fail."

On Monday, January 5, 1981, the *Washington Star* published a short article from the Associated Press:

> President Carter made an emotional farewell appearance yesterday at the Baptist Bible class he has attended for the last four years, saying that humility, compassion, courage and love are qualities that can overcome "broken collar bones and election defeats."
>
> Carter, teaching the class for the last time as president, referred often to his own recent setbacks, and said that if a Christian follows the teachings of Christ and tries hard, "God will understand when you fail."
>
> "How can we expect all of our prayers to be answered when all of Jesus' prayers weren't answered?" Carter said.
>
> He was praised by many members of the class at the First Baptist Church, and Fred Gregg, its regular teacher, said that "In history, in time, people will wake up to what a great president they had."

Three weeks later, on Sunday, January 25, 1981, Ronald Reagan was president of the United States; the hostages held in the U.S. embassy in Iran were free, having been released minutes after Reagan's inauguration; and Jimmy and Rosalynn Carter were at Maranatha Baptist Church in Plains, presenting themselves for membership by transfer of letter from the First Baptist Church of the City of Washington, D.C.

AFTERWORD

Joe Murray was my first newspaper publisher after I graduated from college and joined the staff as a reporter for the Lufkin Daily News *in East Texas. When Joe wrote this column, he was senior writer for Cox Newspapers. Cox subsidized his occasional trips to Washington, D.C., where he would share whiskey and cigars with his good friend, Congressman Charlie Wilson, and —at least once—come to church with me.*

FIRST BAPTIST CHURCH—WASHINGTON STYLE

By Joe Murray
Editor-publisher emeritus of the *Lufkin Daily News*
September 19, 1999

It was Sunday morning in our nation's capital, and I was spending it as I have countless Sundays, boy and man, occupying a pew at the First Baptist Church.

The first time for me at this, the First Baptist of Washington, D.C., but I felt right at home.

Never mind if the surroundings appeared a bit high church for this down-home Southern Baptist.

Ministers in flowing robes ... dueling pulpits, one for Scripture, one for sermonizing ... the choir set off to one side of the altar instead of facing the congregation ... Creeping Methodism was in our midst. ...

Thank goodness when we recited the Lord's Prayer it was the blessed Baptist version, asking for forgiveness of our trespasses as we forgive those who trespass against us, not our debts as we forgive our debtors. That's the one thing the King James is wrong about. Even strict interpretation has its limits.

I read in the church bulletin that the preacher of the day, filling the pulpit in the absence of a full-time pastor, was Dr. James A. Langley, executive director [and] editor emeritus of the D.C. Baptist Convention. A title of nobility, editor emeritus is. I expected the best from his sermon.

Sure enough, we were in the Book of Micah, Chapter 6, Verse 8, as Dr. Langley noted, often considered "the very essence of the Bible."

"And what doth the Lord require of thee, but to do justly, and to love mercy, and to walk humbly with thy God?"

The words may appear so simple, Dr. Langley said, "but they are so demanding."

And while not every Baptist preacher would attempt mixing Mark Twain with Micah, such is the leeway granted editor emerituses. Quoting Mr. Clemens:

"It's not what I don't understand in the Bible that troubles me," Dr. Langley declared. "It's what I do understand."

So it was that the preacher would have us to understand the enormity of the task prescribed:

"God does not merely require justice and mercy, but that we love mercy," he said.

This in a nation that discriminates in employment, in housing for minorities, in pay for women, in capital murder convictions where the accused is later found to be innocent, in stricter penalties for certain types of cocaine, in a justice system that favors the rich and punishes the poor, he said.

Dr. Langley, now quoting Thomas Jefferson:

"I tremble for my country when I reflect that God is just."

And for those of us who would seek to walk with Him:

"He is holy, we are sinful. ... He is almighty, we are frail. ... He is omniscient, and our knowledge is like unto a few grains of sand. ...

"How can we imagine walking with God," Dr. Langley asked, "except with humility?"

We sang a hymn of invitation, we passed the plate, and afterwards we came together in the church basement for a potluck lunch, not so different from different places of worship most everywhere.

It was Sunday morning in our nation's capital—Sunday morning in America.

Joe Murray died Sunday, June 25, 2023, before I could tell him that I was writing a book about Jimmy Carter and my church. Joe had given me permission to reprint his column about First Baptist D.C. when the church celebrated its 220th anniversary in 2022, but I never got it posted to the church website. Lucky me.

This book is the right place for Joe's column for two reasons. First, Jimmy Carter took the oath of office at his inauguration with his hand on a Bible open to Micah 6:8—the same scripture Joe heard at First Baptist:

"And what doth the Lord require of thee, but to do justly, and to love mercy, and to walk humbly with thy God?"

Second, Joe's closing line is the perfect coda to the story of a president and a family who found normal lives at First Baptist D.C.:

It was Sunday morning in our nation's capital—Sunday morning in America.

ACKNOWLEDGMENTS

I'm going to forget to acknowledge someone, so I'll just apologize right now.

I am grateful for the four years that Jimmy Carter was an active member of my church and the gift of his time, wisdom and inspiration.

Generous permissions made this book possible, and I thank the members and leaders of First Baptist D.C.; the staff of the Jimmy Carter Presidential Library and their counterparts at the Harry S. Truman Presidential Library; the Disability Rights Defense and Education Fund; Judson Press; Edward Hughes Pruden Jr.; Janis Johnson; and Betsy Porter Groves, whose father's diary was the spark that started me on this project. As a longtime note-taker, I extend special appreciation to the White House aides who maintained the official presidential daily diary. The details of President Carter's days added important insight to the narratives.

The story of Jimmy Carter and First Baptist D.C. would be full of holes without the research and organization of Our Ladies of the Archives: Janice Osborn, Ellen Parkhurst and Sadye Doxie. The history that they and their predecessors have preserved isn't just that of a 222-year-old church; it's the history of Washington, D.C.

My thanks to every friend, family member and random acquaintance who listened to me talk about this project. I especially appreciate the encouragement of my colleagues in the Society of Professional Journalists. You helped more than you could ever know.

Finally, this book wouldn't be a book without the wizardry of the woman behind the curtain, editor, coach and formatting queen Cyndi Hughes of Booktique Consulting in Austin, Texas. This was a wonderful romp.

SOURCES

Since my earliest years as a newspaper reporter, I've avoided reading almost anything written about the same topic I'm researching. I will read original sources, such as court decisions, speech texts (when I haven't heard the speeches myself) or diary entries, but I rarely read other writers' work on the subject. I don't want their conclusions or words to interfere with mine.

That said, I drew insights from a few published works that I list here. If I quoted from them, I cite the source in the text or the endnotes, because I passionately hate footnotes. Those little super-script distractions may be necessary in legal documents, but they're no good in a narrative.[1]

I glanced at the indexes of two biographies to find out if First Baptist D.C. was mentioned in connection with President Jimmy Carter. I didn't find a reference, which made me more determined to write this book.

---

1. See? I told you footnotes are distracting. If I had anything important to say here, I would have put it in the text. Plus, there's no No. 2. That's a violation by itself. Now go back to reading.

BIBLIOGRAPHY

Jimmy Carter, *White House Diary*, Farrar, Straus and Giroux. 2010

John DeFerrari and Douglas Peter Sefton, *Sixteenth Street NW: Washington, DC's Avenue of Ambitions*, Georgetown University Press, 2022

Bruce T. Gourley, *A Capsule History of Baptists*, Baptist History and Heritage Society, 2010

Edward Hughes Pruden, *Building the House of God: Some Memories*, First Baptist Church of the City of Washington D.C., 1986

Edward Hughes Pruden, *Interpreters Needed: The Eternal Gospel and Our Contemporary Society*, Judson Press, 1951

Edward Hughes Pruden, *A Window on Washington*, Vantage Press Inc., 1976

Edward Hughes Pruden, Windows pamphlet, First Baptist Church of the City of Washington D.C. undated

Dorothy Clark Winchcole, *The First Baptists in Washington, D.C.: 1802-1952*, First Baptist Church of the City of Washington, D.C., 1952

THE CLOUD OF WITNESSES

Shortly after Jimmy Carter entered hospice care in February 2023, I started talking to people who interacted with him at the First Baptist Church of Washington, D.C., and elsewhere. I am grateful for the time and stories they shared, and I apologize to anyone I talked to and forgot to name.

From the extended church family:

Julie Geren · Fred M. Gregg III · Hall Gregg · Betsy Groves · Kevin Hodges · Sarah Hodges-Austin · Bonnie Jorgensen · Beverley Kennedy · Julie Maplesden · Shirley McBeath · Janice Osborn · Kevin Osborn · Ellen Parkhurst · Wilma Prince · Clark Smith · Ed Sonnenschein · Richard Turner · Susan Whittenberg

From outside the church:

Jerry B. Cain · Tony Clark · Paul Dolinsky · Bill Fitz-Patrick · Janis Johnson · Jim LeBrecht · Carl P. Leubsdorf

ENDNOTES

THE INTROIT

The Campaign
Competing churches: Marjorie Hyer, "The Church for Carter?" *Washington Post*, August 1, 1976
Kiwanis club: Author email interview with Ed Pruden Jr., October 25, 2023
Coveting: "Rival Claims on Carter," Letters to the Editor, *Washington Post*, August 12, 1976

The Prayers
Pre-inaugural prayer: Baptist Press, "Baptist Leaders Pray for President Carter," *Capital Baptist*, DC Baptist Convention, February 3, 1977
Bible verses: King James Version, Bible Gateway
Plains Baptist pastor: Baptist Press, "Bruce Edwards Resigns Plains Baptist Pastorate," *Capital Baptist*, March 3, 1977
Private service: "Pre-Inaugural Services Held at First Baptist Church," *First Baptist Church News*, January 26, 1977

The Invitation
Carters joining First Baptist D.C.:
William F. Willoughby, "Carter Presence Elates Churchgoers," *Washington Star*, January 24, 1977
Letter of Recommendation from Plains Baptist Church, Archives of First Baptist D.C.
Jimmy Carter, *White House Diary*, Farrar, Straus and Giroux, 2010, page 13

The Baptism
Amy Carter Baptism:
Janis Johnson, "Amy Carter Baptized Here: President's Daughter Immersed in Heated Pool," *Washington Post*, February 7, 1977
William F. Willoughby, "Amy Carter's Baptism: She Reached Decision," *Washington Star*, February 7, 1977
Opera escape:
United Press International, "The Carters' Afternoon at the Opera," *Washington Star*, February 7, 1977

THE CHURCH

The Bricks and Mortar
Architecture of First Baptist D.C. and Plains Baptist: Author email interview with Paul Dolinsky, August 24, 2023
Early buildings: Dorothy Clark Winchcole, *The First Baptists in Washington, D.C.: 1802-1952*, pages 4 and 9

First Baptist on 10th Street: "Ford's Theatre: Places," National Park Service (https://www.nps.gov/foth/learn/historyculture/places.htm)

1890 building: John DeFerrari and Douglas Peter Sefton, *Sixteenth Street NW: Washington DC's Avenue of Ambitions,* Georgetown University Press, 2022, pages 57-58

Financing: Edward Hughes Pruden, *Building the House of God: Some Memories* booklet, First Baptist D.C., 1986, pages 8-10

New building: "First Baptist Church Launches $600,000 Building Fund Drive," *Washington Star,* May 3, 1949

The Pews

No pews: Winchcole, *The First Baptists in Washington D.C.,* pages 4-5

Traveling pews: Pruden, *Building the House of God,* pages 15-16

The Windows

Baptists and other Christians: First Baptist D.C., "Rededication of the Stained Glass Windows," pamphlet, November 6, 1988

Sam Houston's baptism: "What were Sam Houston's connections to Baylor University?" Baylor University, July 1, 2016 (https://www2.baylor.edu/baylorproud/2016/07/what-were-sam-houstons-connections-to-baylor-university)

Windows: First Baptist D.C., "Dedicatory Service" program, October 13, 1968

The Pastors

Dismissal of pastor: Marjorie Hyer, "President's Pastor Is Fired by Church in a Stormy Debate," *Washington Post,* October 29, 1979

Trentham's rebuttal: Jim Castelli, "Carter's D.C. Church Fires Pastor, Members Cite 'Poor Judgment,' " *Washington Star,* October 29, 1979

Reverend Cranford: Jimmy Carter, foreword to *Cups of Light and Other Illustrations* by Clarence Cranford, Judson Press, 1988

Death of former pastor: Bob Barrett, "Dr. Trentham, Noted Pastor, Dies in Crash," *Knoxville News-Sentinel,* July 24, 1992

From the Archives: Edward Hughes Pruden, Author's Foreword to *Interpreters Needed: The Eternal Gospel and our Contemporary Society,* copyright 1951, Judson Press, Valley Forge, Pennsylvania. Reprinted with permission.

The Denomination

Baptists in the Rose Garden: Jim Newton, "President Carter Thanks Baptists for Their Prayers," *Capital Baptist,* DC Baptist Convention, May 26, 1977

Election of Jimmy Carter: Foreign Missions Board, 132nd Annual, Southern Baptist Convention

Moral Majority: Carter, *White House Diary,* page 485

Moderates withhold cash:

Mary Jacoby, "Texas Pastor Leads Collection Plate Revolt by Moderate Baptists," *Washington Post,* September 1, 1990

R. Gustav Niebuhr, "Many Southern Baptists May Withhold Large Sums from Conservative Coffers," *Wall Street Journal,* August 24, 1990

Baptist Faith & Message: Baptist Faith & Message 2000, Southern Baptist Convention (SBC) (https://bfm.sbc.net/bfm2000/)

Carter quits Southern Baptist Convention: "Letter From Jimmy Carter," Texas Baptists Committed (https://www.txbc.org/2000Journals/Oct2000/Oct00letterfromjimmyc.htm)

THE STEEPLE

President Truman's suggestions: Pruden, *A Window on Washington,* page 66

THE PEOPLE

The Multitudes
Crowds: Janis Johnson, "Carter Church All Astir: Tourists, Agents, Press Upset 1st Baptist," *Washington Post,* June 17, 1977
Visitors coffee: "Some Change Called For," *First Baptist Church News,* February 9, 1977
Visitor's letter: Letter, *First Baptist Church News,* January 17, 1978
Visiting pharmacist: Typed letter, May 8, 1978, First Baptist D.C. archives
No autographs: Charles R. Sanks Jr., letter, May 18, 1978, First Baptist D.C. archives
William Jewell students: Author interview with Jerry B. Cain, July 12, 2024

The Predecessors
President Johnson and Billy Graham: United Press International, "LBJ Takes Graham to Baptist Services," *Washington Post,* September 12, 1966
President Jefferson letter: "From Thomas Jefferson to Obadiah B. Brown, 17 October 1808," (This is an early access document from the papers of Thomas Jefferson. It is not an authoritative final version.) Founders Online, National Archives (https://founders.archives.gov/documents/Jefferson/99-01-02-8877)
President Harding: Winchcole, *The First Baptists in Washington, D.C.,* page 18
President Hoover: Unknown Washington newspaper article, D.C. Public Library
President Truman message: Robert Tate Allan, "Baptists to Hear Truman Letter," *Washington Daily News,* June 30, 1951
President Johnson: Christi Harlan, *Mr. President, The Class Is Yours: Jimmy Carter's Sunday School Lessons in Washington, D.C.,* Christi Harlan Media, LLC, 2024, page 62
LBJ award: Press release announcing the 2016 LBJ Liberty & Justice for All Award to former President Jimmy Carter, LBJ Foundation, January 13, 2016 (https://lbjaward.org/2016-liberty-justice-award.html)
President Carter's affinity with Truman: Jim Williams, "Oral History Interview with Jimmy and Rosalynn Carter," Oral History #1991-29, October 1991, National Park Service(https://www.nps.gov/articles/000/jimmy-carter-oral-history-interview.htm)

The Presidential Party
Griffin Bell: Membership card, First Baptist D.C. archives
Mary Prince Fitzpatrick: United Press International, "Amy's Nurse a Step Away From Becoming a Baptist," *Washington Star,* March 21, 1977
Mika Brzezinski: Presidential Daily Diary, entry for September 23, 1979, Jimmy Carter Presidential Library (https://www.jimmycarterlibrary.gov/research/daily-diary?selected_year_month=197909&selected_year=1979)
John C. White: Memorial service program, January 31, 1995, First Baptist D.C. archives
Joining First Baptist: Caspar Nannes, "First Baptist Celebrates 176th Anniversary," *First Baptist Church News,* May 17, 1978

John C. White biography: Handbook of Texas, Texas State Historical Association website, November 22, 2013, updated August 3, 2020 (https://www.tshaonline.org/handbook/entries/white-john-coyle)

The Press

Carter's address at White House Correspondents Association dinner: Office of the White House Press Secretary, Remarks of the President at the White House Correspondents Dinner, Washington Hilton Hotel, April 30, 1977

Carter's reaction to WHCA: Carter, *White House Diary,* page 192

Covering Carter at church: Janis Johnson, "At DC's First Baptist Church With President Jimmy Carter," *WomanTraveler,* September 24, 2023 (https://womantraveler.info/at-dcs-first-baptist-church-with-president-jimmy-carter/)

Death of Caspar Nannes: "In Grateful Memory of Caspar Nannes," *First Baptist Church News,* December 6, 1978

The Guardians

Mildred New: Kenneth A. Briggs, "Capital Church Wants Carter to Feel at Home," *New York Times,* January 20, 1977

Secret Service: "Cranny: Going Like Sixty at Seventy-five," *American Baptist People,* Volume 4: 1981, pages 6-8

After worship: The Executive Protective Service, formerly the White House Police Force, was part of the Secret Service. It was renamed the U.S. Secret Service Uniformed Division on November 15, 1977 (https://www.secretservice.gov/about/history/timeline)

The Laying on of Hands

"Policies for Demonstrators," undated, First Baptist D.C. archives

Kick in the ass: Sally Quinn, "2 Booted Out in Church Demonstration," *Washington Post,* October 3, 1977

Nuclear oversight: Alice Buck, "A History of the Energy Development and Research Administration," U.S. Department of Energy, March 1982 (https://www.energy.gov/sites/prod/files/ERDA%20History.pdf)

Neutron bomb: "Press and the Neutron Bomb: Summary Intro," Harvard Kennedy School, February 1, 1984 (https://case.hks.harvard.edu/press-and-the-neutron-bomb-summary-intro/)

The Nuclear Option

Protesters: B.D. Colen, "Five Arrested in Protest at Carter Church," *Washington Post,* October 17, 1977

First atomic bombing: "Marching to Victory: The Bombing of Hiroshima, August 6, 1945," Truman Library Institute (https://www.trumanlibraryinstitute.org/wwii-75-marching-victory-18/)

Protesters' statement: William F. Willoughby, "9 Arrested in Church After Rapping Carter on Nuclear Policy," *Washington Star,* August 7, 1978

Order to bomb: "Marching to Victory," Truman Library Institute (https://www.trumanlibraryinstitute.org/wwii-75-marching-victory-18/)

The 504 Demonstrators

Crip Camp: A Disability Revolution, directed, written and produced by James LeBrecht and Nicole Newnham, 2020

We Shall Not be Moved: The 504 Sit-In for Disability Civil Rights, audio documentary produced by Asata Iman, 1997, Disability Rights Education & Defense Fund (DREDF) (https://dredf.org/we-shall-not-be-moved/)

"Confronting the D.C. Power," 1977, Disability Rights and Education Fund (DREDF) (https://dredf.org/confronting-the-d-c-power/)

State of the Union remarks: Jimmy Carter State of the Union Address, January 16, 1981, Jimmy Carter Presidential Library & Museum (https://www.jimmycarterlibrary.gov/the-carters/selected-speeches/jimmy-carter-state-of-the-union-address-1981)

THE SUNDAY SCHOOL CLASS

The Couples Class

History of the Couples Class: Unknown author, First Baptist D.C. archives

Carter's first class as teacher: United Press International, "Carter Teaches His 1st Church Class in District," *Washington Post*, February 21, 1977

First Sunday School in D.C.: Winchcole, *The First Baptists in Washington, D.C.*, page 6

From the Archives: Caspar Nannes, "The President as Teacher," *First Baptist Church News*, April 12, 1977

The Banquet

Carter's state dinners: "All the Presidents' Meals" infographic, Foreign Policy (https://foreignpolicy.com/all-the-presidents-meals-state-dinners-white-house-infographic/)

Couples Class banquet: Caspar Nannes, "Even a President Needs Love: President & Mrs. Carter Attend Church Banquet," *Capital Baptist*, November 10, 1977

THE TEACHERS

The Substitute

Fred Gregg's humor: William F. Willoughby, "Sterile Egg? Or Is the Incubator at Fault?" *Washington Star*, August 12, 1978

Funny dialogue: Transcripts of Sunday School classes recorded at First Baptist D.C. Used with permission of First Baptist D.C.

The Troublesome Book

Revelation: John, New Testament, the Bible

The Missionary

Fred Gregg interview: Lawrence McQuillan, United Press International, "Missionary Career Ahead for Carter?" *Washington Star*, January 29, 1978

Baptist missionaries: Carter, *White House Diary*, pages 35 and 41

White House meeting: Baptist Press, 'President Urges Volunteer Mission Program," *Capital Baptist*, DC Baptist Convention, June 23, 1977

Missionary proposal: Annual of the Southern Baptist Convention 1977, page 40 (http://media2.sbhla.org.s3.amazonaws.com/annuals/SBC_Annual_1977.pdf)

Proposal abandoned: Carter, *White House Diary*, page 35

THE LESSONS IN THE BALCONY

The Reader
Rosalynn Carter's duties: Carter, *White House Diary*, page 25
Amy's tooth: Doug Porter, diary, June 18, 1978, First Baptist D.C. archives
Award from American Public Health Association: "Our History," American Public Health Association (https://www.apha.org/about-apha/our-history)
From the Archives: The Disasters
Toccoa Falls flood: "Flood of November 6, 1977," TFC History (https://tfchistory.com/photos/flood-of-november-6-1977/)
First Lady's role: Carter, *White House Diary*, page 121
First Lady's remarks: "At Least 37 Die as Earthen Dam Bursts in Georgia," *Washington Post*, November 7, 1977
Flood debris: B. Drummond Ayres Jr., "Bible School Dean Sees God's Plan in Disaster," *New York Times*, November 8, 1977
Creation of FEMA:
Federal Emergency Management Agency Message to the Congress Transmitting Reorganization Plan No. 3 of 1978, The American Presidency Project (ucsb.edu)
Executive Order 12148—Federal Emergency Management, The American Presidency Project (https://www.presidency.ucsb.edu/documents/executive-order-12148-federal-emergency-management)
Disaster declarations: "Disasters and Other Declarations," Federal Emergency Management Agency (https://www.fema.gov/disaster/declarations)

The Christian, the Muslim and the Jew
Associated Press, "Carter Takes the Day Off; Wins Bible Class Ovation," *Washington Star*, September 25, 1978
Prayer service:
Baptist Press, "Pres. Carter's Church Launches 'Meeting of Peacemakers,' " *Capital Baptist*, November 15, 1978
"Service of Prayers Held at First Baptist for Camp David Summit," *First Baptist Church News*, September 20, 1978
Sunday School remarks:
Harlan, *Mr. President, The Class Is Yours*, pages 71-72

The Baptist from Kyiv
Pastor Georgi Vins: John Bloom, "Let My People Pray," *Texas Monthly*, August 1979
Vins' release:
Edward Walsh, "5 Dissidents Freed by Soviets," *Washington Post*, April 28, 1979
Jody Powell announcement, Public Papers of the Presidents, volume 1, page 731.
Vins at First Baptist D.C.:
Baptist Press, "Just-Freed Georgi Vins Worships With the Carters at Washington's First Baptist," *Capital Baptist*, DC Baptist Convention, May 24, 1979
Carter, *White House Diary*, page 317
Marjorie Hyer, "President Likens Soviet Dissident to Bible Figure," *Washington Post*, April 30, 1979

The Vote

From the Archives: "A Message of Love and Support for President and Mrs. Carter,"
    November 12, 1980, First Baptist D.C. archives
Carter thank-you: First Baptist Church News, December 24, 1980

The Final Lesson

President Carter's broken collarbone: Norman D. Sandler, "Carter Recuperates From
    Broken Collarbone; Meets Algerians," UPI Archives, December 28, 1980 (https://
    www.upi.com/Archives/1980/12/28/Carter-recuperates-from-broken-collarbone-
    meets-Algerians/3411346827600/print/)
Last class: Associated Press, "Carter Teaches Last Class Here," *Washington Star,* January
    5, 1981

AFTERWORD

Joe Murray, "First Baptist Church—Washington Style," *Lufkin Daily News,* September
    19, 1999
Inaugural Bible: Baptist Press, "Carter's Inaugural Address Based on Biblical
    Concepts," Capital Baptist, February 3, 1977

INDEX

This is an incomplete index. I omitted the names of people who are mentioned frequently, including lead Sunday School teacher Fred Gregg, usher Doug Porter, pastor emeritus Edward Hughes Pruden Sr. and journalists Marjorie Hyer, Janis Johnson, Caspar Nannes and William F. Willoughby.

Consider this less of an index and more of an appetizer menu. The main dish and some specials are in the text.

ABOUT THE AUTHOR

Christi Harlan is a writer and communications consultant in Washington, D.C. During a 20-year career as a reporter, her articles appeared on the front pages of the *Wall Street Journal*, the *Dallas Morning News* and the *Austin American-Statesman*.

After newspapers, she held top communications jobs at the Senate Banking Committee, the Federal Emergency Management Agency, the Securities and Exchange Commission and the Public Company Accounting Oversight Board.

Beginning with Hurricane Katrina, Christi spent six years as a volunteer and consultant in disaster public affairs with the American Red Cross, providing media interviews and writing eyewitness accounts of the Red Cross's response to hurricanes, ice storms, flooding and the deadly tornadoes in Enterprise, Alabama, and Joplin, Missouri.

A native of Manhattan, Kansas, Christi attended junior and senior high school in Houston and earned a bachelor's degree in journalism and English from Stephen F. Austin State University in Nacogdoches, Texas. She was accepted to the Knight Fellowship in Law for

Journalists and earned a Master of Studies in Law from Yale Law School.

In August 1993, Christi joined the First Baptist Church of the City of Washington, D.C., where her journalistic skills of taking notes and writing suited the jobs of church clerk and volunteer communications director. She is owned by two cats who think every computer screen is occupied by magical nests of squirrels.

Follow me here:

www.christiharlanwriter.com
christi@christiharlanwriter.com

 linkedin.com/in/christiharlan

WANT TO READ MORE?

The companion volume to this book is *Mr. President, The Class Is Yours,* containing previously unpublished transcripts of 14 Sunday School lessons that Jimmy Carter taught at First Baptist D.C. while he was president.

If you've already bought and read the book, thank you! If you enjoyed it, please take a moment to write a review when you go online to order gift copies for your family and friends.

If you haven't read *Mr. President,* I hope the excerpts quoted in this book will inspire you to seek out the words of a great Bible teacher who just happened to be President of the United States.

Here's the opening of President Carter's lesson on his final Sunday with the Couples Class at First Baptist D.C. I will testify that the end of the lesson is as good as the beginning, but you don't have to take my word for it. Go get *Mr. President, The Class Is Yours* from your favorite bookseller.

FROM *MR. PRESIDENT, THE CLASS IS YOURS*

January 4, 1981

"We're going to be living a good Christian life and staying close to all of you, cherishing the friendships and the memories. We hope to come back and visit you as often as possible. ... [O]ne of the finest things that ever happened to us, personally, was the joining of this class and the friendship with Fred Gregg and all of you who've accepted us, not as a public official in some ivory tower, but as a human being, as a fellow Christian, and as a friend.

"We've never come into this class when we were treated with anything other than genuine fellowship and friendship, and on a personal basis. And it really meant a lot to us in a trying position of being president of this great country. We've also never had any unpleasant experiences in this church; everything has been fine for us.

"And I know that the church has been through trying times. ... But I know that the church has been a strong one and a symbol of commitment and courage and dedication in this nation's capital for many generations. And I know it will continue to be that in the future.

"We will be going home to Plains immediately after the inaugural ceremonies. We'll walk around the other side of the Capitol, get on a helicopter, fly to Andrews Air Force Base and take off to Warner

Robins, Georgia. And then we'll go on down to Plains from there. And we'll be living a good, private life. We'll join the church in Plains, and I expect to be as active or maybe even more so than I have been in this Sunday School.

"When we haven't been here on Sunday mornings, we've been to church at Camp David. We ordinarily invited the chaplain from a nearby military base to come in to give us a private church service. And then on special days, we've had several hundred military personnel there for Thanksgiving, Christmas services and so forth. But we've kept our ties with this church even on Sundays that we weren't here. ...

"We have a responsibility this morning to, I think, forget about goings and comings of class members and revert back to the teaching of the Bible. And if all of you would turn to Luke 9, I'll let you help me with the lesson."

Mr. President, The Class Is Yours
Now available here

https://books2read.com/mrpresidentclass